I QUIT SUGAR

with Sarah Wilson

KIDS' COOKBOOK

I QUIT SUGAR

with *Sarah Wilson*

KIDS'
COOKBOOK

EASY AND FUN
SUGAR-FREE RECIPES
FOR YOUR LITTLE
PEOPLE!

bluebird
books for life

Me and my nose-kissing little friend Saskia.

Me and my mate's cheeky kids.

My goddaughter Charlotte who loves fermented cucumbers!

(Who I seem to only visit in my bikini!)

CONTENTS

My mate Lizzy's little charmer.

INTRODUCTION

Mums and dads around the world want to ease their kids off sugar.
But *how* to do it?

Since I first quit sugar back in January 2011 (goodness, it's been that long!), more than 1 million people have followed my 8-Week Programme and book to successfully come off the white stuff, experiencing a wellness, energy and natural appetite they haven't had since, well, they were kids.

The challenge now, for both myself and parents out there, is our children – getting them well, energised and happily sugar free. It's a challenge the I Quit Sugar team and I are fully up for!

The food we eat and the way we eat it has changed radically in the past generation. So much so, kids today don't experience the kind of wellness, energy and natural appetite (free of sugar highs and lows) that I believe they're entitled to. The sugar industry targets kids, aware that if they can shift children's palates now, they'll have captive consumers for life. Kids tend to gravitate – actually they're lured – towards snack foods, foods with crunch and foods that come in packets, AKA foods that come laden with sugar. Parents are busier than ever and resort to food that's easy to dump into a lunchbox without fuss. Again, food brimful of sugar.

So, how to get our kids off sugar?!

I'll be getting my hair cut, buying loo paper at the supermarket or climbing out of my local pool and a parent will come up to tell me how deeply concerned they are about their kids' eating habits and the way sugar is impacting their health and behaviour. Sometimes they're in tears, totally fed up and feeling like failures. It brings me to tears.

Parents feel guilty that they're doing the wrong thing by their kids.

Parents feel powerless to change their situation. The competing food messages, the hidden sugars they're not told about, the way their kids are 'sold to', the kids' parties they don't want to shut their kids off from . . .

Meanwhile, our kids are feeling addicted. And compromised.

All of which has motivated me and the I Quit Sugar team to write this book.

I don't have kids; I have nephews, 'little friends' (my mates' children) and godchildren. And I've spoken to a lot of parents in toilet-paper aisles and pool change rooms over the past few years.

My feeling is that things can be simpler than we're making it . . . and kinder.

As many of you who have done my 8-Week Programme know, going sugar free is not about miserably following a mean, restrictive diet.

Eating sugar free is about abundance and 'crowding out'. It's not about 'bad' foods and banning certain items. Instead, we focus on eating a whole stack of other (sugarless) snacks, treats and meals so there simply isn't enough room left for the sugary stuff.

With kids, this means making savoury foods fun and exciting.

Eating sugar free is about dense nutrition. Quitting sugar isn't just about eliminating sugar. It's also – at its core – about taking things back to the way our grandparents ate, before the advent of Type 2 diabetes and obesity, and the rest. It's about eating whole foods. It's about getting as many nutrients into our gullets as possible.

For kids, this means injecting meals with veggies (without them necessarily noticing!) and plenty of great protein and healthy fats.

Eating sugar free is about eating less ingredients and packet free. Sometimes I feel this is the simplest advice I can give: when choosing what to eat, go for the version of a food with the least number of ingredients. Plain oats are better than breakfast cereals with 27 ingredients, for instance. Another way to go about things: avoid things in packets. When you go sugar free it mostly cuts to this same chase.

And perhaps most importantly . . .

Eating sugar free is about being gentle and kind. We don't do harsh edicts. We make this fun and positive.

We ease our kids into this, encouraging their good habits.

I don't necessarily recommend kids do the 8-Week Programme. Instead, I suggest kids are weaned off sugar slowly and with absolutely no fuss or stigma. Making it fun helps. Getting them more engaged with good food helps even more. Giving them healthy takes on food they love is another proven trick. This book focuses squarely on these principles. All recipes are injected with as many veggies as we could get away with, most are designed to be cooked with your kids and all of them are fun. We also invited a few sugar-free parents in our orbit to share a tip or recipe or two, just to mix it up a bit.

So how to get our kids off sugar? Fret less and start cooking!

Much wellness to you and your family,

Sarah
xx

PS If you'd like to know more about quitting sugar, and try out more kid-friendly recipes, check out IQuitSugar.com.

SHOULD MY KIDS BE SUGAR FREE?

Yeah, we reckon so.

Let's start here. Kids aged 4–8 should be consuming no more than 3 teaspoons of sugar a day. These are the recommendations from the World Health Organization.

That sounds reasonable, and manageable, right?

Well, here's the scary truth.

- A large glass of apple juice contains 8–10 teaspoons of sugar – the same as a can of Coke.

- The average bowl of cereal has 3 teaspoons of sugar.

- A slice of white toast with jam has 4 teaspoons of sugar.

Our kids are eating 3–4 times the recommended daily intake, and that's before they leave the breakfast table!

Why should we be concerned?

Well, here's what sugar does to kids:

- Sugar alters the palate. Studies have shown that sugar strips the body of vital nutrients, and in particular zinc. Zinc is essential in the development of taste and palate in young children.

- Sugar causes mood disorders. Kids who eat diets high in refined sugar are more likely to suffer from depression, anxiety and mood disorders.

- Sugar makes kids fat. 25 per cent of Australian children are overweight or obese.

- Sugar causes behavioural problems. High-sugar diets inhibit the body's ability to absorb vital nutrients, resulting in the body being deficient in micronutrients. These deficiencies (particularly iron) have been linked to behavioural disorders – like ADHD – in young children.

- Sugar inhibits the immune system. Sugar destroys the functions of bacteria, fighting white blood cells and wreaking havoc for up to five hours after ingestion. It also interferes with the absorption of Vitamin C, one of the essential nutrients for immune function.

- Sugar makes kids aggressive. See page 3 for the hard facts.

- Sugar affects memory. Studies show that kids who consume sugary drinks could suffer from poor memory function throughout adulthood.

SOFT DRINKS: THE STICKY TRUTH

Research has found the more sugary drinks a child consumes, the worse their behaviour is likely to be. Coincidence? No.

A two-month study by Columbia University was done on five-year-olds, monitoring how many sugary drinks they had a day, as well as how their behaviour was over the same period.

- Almost half of the 3000 children involved drank one can of soft drink a day.

- More than 120 had four – or more – glasses of the toxic stuff each day.

- The link between soft drinks and aggression was cited as 'strong and consistent.'

But what about fruit?

We're glad you asked.

We're not suggesting you strip fruit from your kids' diet. Kids are growing little humans who need a wide variety of whole foods. However, some fruit is very high in natural sugar and low in fibre, and for that reason we have preferences for fruits at the other end of the scale.

One or two serves of low-fructose fruit daily is perfect, eaten with some protein and fat to slow the absorption of the sugar (apple slices with cheese; berries with nuts). We tend to opt for fruits high in fibre as well.

EAT MORE	EAT LESS
kiwi fruits	bananas
raspberries	apples
blueberries	pears
grapefruits	mangoes
lemons	grapes
peaches	cherries

WHAT SHOULD MY KIDS BE EATING EVERY DAY?

For a rundown on Australian dietary guidelines for children visit nhmrc.gov.au.

If you're after the USA guidelines visit cnpp.usda.gov and if you're after the UK guidelines visit food.gov.uk.

Guidelines are great. But many nutritionists and health experts argue they tend to contain too many grains and carbs and not enough greens. We agree.

Sarah's mantra has always been:

- To ensure there is plenty of protein and fat with every meal.
- To pack in as many veggies – particularly leafy greens – into your kids' meals as possible.

Our own guidelines

VEGETABLES

For kids aged 2–4 try to include 3–4 serves of veggies a day.

For kids aged 5–13 try to include 5 serves of veggies a day.

Always opt for dark leafy greens over other greens over starchy vegetables (such as peas, corn and carrots).

Here's what 5 serves of vegetables looks like:

½ medium

1 medium

3 cups (about 300 g)

½ cup (75 g)

PROTEIN

For kids aged 2–4 try to include 2–3 serves of protein a day.

For kids aged 5–13 try to include 3 serves of protein a day.

Choose unseasoned fish fillets, eggs and organic meat over fried, battered or marinated varieties.

Here's what 3 serves of protein looks like:

100 g   100 g   2 large

DAIRY

Kids aged 2–7 need 1½ serves a day.

Kids aged 8–12 need 3 serves a day.

Choose full-fat, unflavoured milk, cheese and yoghurt over flavoured varieties with added fruit.

Here's what 3 serves of dairy looks like:

1 cup (250 ml)   2 slices   ¾ cup (175 ml)

If you're wondering what your kids' lunchbox should look like we've broken it down for you on page 80.

DID YOU KNOW?

You can get zippy with ZINC.

Zinc is essential for developing the palate. It also increases immunity and balances blood sugar levels. It may interest you to know that kids with low zinc levels have much higher incidences of food allergies.

Zinc is – ironically – mostly found in sugar-free foods (like nuts, beef, spinach and seeds). Sugar depletes zinc. Ergo, when your child eats lots of sugar their ability to recognise new and unique flavours is compromised. In addition, it messes with their immunity and wreaks havoc on their blood sugar levels. Keep feeding your kids sugar-free foods and their zinc levels will be right on track.

Can my baby be sugar free?

In a nutshell: yes.

Whether your baby has been breast-fed or bottle-fed, they've had little exposure to processed, refined sugars. As you start to wean them, you might like to follow our nifty guide below to help work out when to allow a few sweet foods at a pace that won't see them become addicted.

When can my baby have sweet food?

We asked Accredited Practising Dietitian Natalie Bourke to help pull this together.

AGE	FOOD SUGGESTION	NOTES
4–6 months	avocado egg yolk banana sweet potato	Try soft boiling an egg yolk and puree with some avocado. This is a great nutrient dense first food.
6–8 months	squash with cinnamon pureed/lumpy meat, fish and chicken* coconut yoghurt herbs and spices	Babies begin to lose their iron stores from about 6 months on. This is a great time to introduce iron-rich foods such as mince, chicken and fish.
8–12 months	minced/fork tender meat, and fish and chicken* buttered sweet potato fries soft carrot sticks with guacamole	Pairing your baby's vegetables and fruit with a healthy fat source such as butter, coconut oil or avocado helps your baby absorb the fat-soluble vitamins contained in the fruit and vegetables.
12+ months	Finger foods and family foods: Check out the recipes in this book for great nourishing dishes to feed your growing baby.	At this stage kids can eat what you are eating. Always focus on unprocessed food, and let them get messy – using all of their fine motor skills is super important!

* Each child progresses at varying speeds through tolerating different textures, so use your discretion and consult with your healthcare provider if you are concerned.

ALLERGY SUBSTITUTION GUIDE

If your kids can't eat nuts:

WHOLE-NUT ALTERNATIVES

- **Seeds** – pumpkin, sunflower and sesame seeds are easy to eat on the go or add to dishes calling for nuts. They are also rich in protein, vitamins, minerals and essential fatty acids.
- **Toasted coconut flakes** – nut free and delicious, a great crunchy topper for any dish. We use these a lot throughout this book.

NUT-MEAL ALTERNATIVES

- **Buckwheat flour** – technically a fruit, but acts like a grain, rich in manganese, tryptophan and magnesium.
- **Coconut flour** – a great alternative to nut meals but be mindful to add moisture or eggs as it absorbs any moisture.
- **Spelt flour** – this ancient grain has a nut-like flavour, so is a great substitute (this flour contains gluten).

If your kids can't eat gluten:

FLOUR ALTERNATIVES

- **Buckwheat flour** – this flour is full of nutrients that contribute to blood sugar control.
- **Coconut flour** – remember to add extra liquid or eggs when using coconut flour as it slurps up moisture quite readily.
- **Almond meal or flour** (or other nut meal or flour) – use a store-bought variety or make your own.
- **Quinoa flakes or flour** – an ancient grain from South America rich in protein, vitamins and minerals.
- **Rice flour** – a basic grain and gluten-free substitute for wheat flour.

If your kids can't eat bread:

Opt for the lowest sugar options in each of the below.

- **Millet bread**
- **Buckwheat bread**
- **Chia bread**
- **Store-bought gluten-free bread**

If your kids can't eat dairy:

YOGHURT/MILK/CHEESEALTERNATIVES

- **Goat's or sheep's milk/yoghurt/cheese** – often people who are intolerant to dairy products can manage goat's or sheep's milk.
- **Coconut milk** – coconut milk or cream can be added to most recipes that call for dairy milk. It can also be used instead of yoghurt in the breakfast chapter (see page 27). Remember to choose the full-fat kind with just coconut and water, no added nasties.
- **Coconut yoghurt** – there are a few of these on the market now that are completely dairy free. Choose the plain kind and add your own extras. It is rich so serve to kids in small doses.
- **Almond milk** – this is super easy to make yourself and substitutes quite well for dairy in recipes or by itself.

BUTTER ALTERNATIVES

- **Ghee** – also known as clarified butter, ghee has the nourishing fats of butter without the allergenic proteins or lactose. Note: as this is derived from butter, it may not be a suitable substitute if your child is very sensitive to dairy.
- **Coconut oil** – completely dairy free and super nutritious.

LET'S GET CRACKING

This chapter is all about how to ease your kids off sugar. We've laid it out in five easy steps.

1. Don't stigmatise sugar

In our experience the best way to get people off sugar (that's big and little people) is to not make a big deal of it. Instead, treat it like a gentle experiment.

Banning or restricting a food often makes it more of a temptation to your kids. 'Forbidden' foods sound super exciting, much like touching a 'Wet Paint!' sign. Highlighting the wet paint (or in this case the triple choc fudge brownie) makes them focus on it and want to grab at it.

Our motto is that it's always better to replace rather than restrict.

Talk about food as fuel to keep bodies healthy, rather than referring to food as 'bad' or discussing restrictive eating. When all else fails, appeal to your kids' imagination by giving fun names to their meals or telling them their greens will make them strong like the Hulk and other superheroes. Focus on fun, not 'bad foods' and 'should nots'.

DID YOU KNOW?

Kids need food every 3–4 hours. Kids need to eat regularly to maintain a blood glucose concentration high enough to support the activity of their brain and nervous system. The brain is the chief glucose consumer, and while a child's brain is as big as an adult's, it's the liver – responsible for storing glucose and releasing it into the blood – that is far smaller in a child and only has the capacity to store around 4 hours' worth of glucose at a time.

2. Be prepared

1. Quit buying packaged food. Aim for your kids' diet to be 80 per cent whole food.

2. Rearrange your store cupboard. Put treat foods out of reach and out of view.

3. Mix it up where possible. Don't get your kids hooked on just one dish. Keep them interested in food with a variety of flavours.

4. Planning is key. Have a bunch of ready-to-go meals and snacks in your fridge, freezer and larder for when the kids are hankering for a quick fix. Use recipes from the Rainy Day Kitchen Fun chapter (see page 67) to help you get prepared for the week ahead.

Try batch-freezing.
Prepare meals in advance and freeze in portions so when you're pressed for time you can easily serve up something nutritious for dinner.

Get ready for the week ahead with this sample of a Weekend Cook-Up:

- Roasted Root Vegetable Crisps (see page 104): Store in an airtight container for up to 4 days in the fridge.

- Activated nuts and seeds: Divvy out nuts and seeds into portions for the week. Have a stash in the freezer. Every day take out a pack and allow nuts to defrost in lunchboxes or your bag until needed.

- Coconut and Raspberry Loaf (see page 73): Freeze in portions or slice and refrigerate in an airtight container for 4 to 5 days.

- Dino Cookie Bites (see page 71): Place one in lunchboxes as a healthy treat or keep a few in a ziplock bag for a snack before soccer practice.

Feeling overwhelmed?

Start small. Swap junky snacks and cereals for healthy options. For example, make your own Sugar-free Cacao Pops (see page 36) to replace store-bought cereals and eliminate soft drinks. These two small changes will dramatically improve your kids' health.

3. Take the kids shopping

Ask the kids to find three items on your shopping list in the supermarket. Engaging them in choosing, sorting and finding foods will help them recognise different varieties of fruit and veg, and teach them to select the best options off the shelves.

DID YOU KNOW?

The average baby yoghurt has 16 ingredients in it.

The second of which, in many cases, is sugar (ingredients are listed in descending order of volume).

SKIM MILK, SUGAR, BANANA (MIN. 5%), WATER, CREAM, MILK SOLIDS, THICKENER (1442), MINERAL CALCIUM (341, 333), HALAL GELATINE, FRUCTOSE, VEGETABLE GUMS (440, 406), NATURAL FLAVOURS, ACIDITY REGULATORS (330, 331), NATURAL COLOUR (160b), VITAMIN D, LIVE YOGHURT CULTURES (S.THERMOPHILUS, L.BULGARICUS, L.ACIDOPHILUS, B.LACTIS).

Try this instead: Buy full-fat unsweetened natural yoghurt and stir through a ¼ mashed banana. That's 13 ingredients less than the one above!

4. Get the kids growing

Every expert we've spoken to agrees that when kids actively grow their own veggies they're more likely to eat them, too. It's a win all round!

MAKE CHIA HEADS

- 2 teaspoons chia seeds
- 2–3 handfuls potting mix
- empty eggshells
- eggcups
- acrylic paint

Wash the empty eggshells thoroughly under warm running water, removing any membrane stuck to the inside. Fill with some soil and sprinkle the chia seeds on top of the soil. Spray thoroughly with water (you can use a garden spray) and leave for 5–6 days (not in direct sun), spraying the seeds lightly each day. By day 6–7 the seeds will be ready to eat. Meanwhile, paint some eggcups with miniature outfits. Feel free to add limbs and other accoutrements. Give each one a name. 'Hey, look, Maria's sprouting!'

MAKE A SALAD BOWL PATCH

- 2 tablespoons seeds (lettuce, herbs, spinach, radish)
- old salad bowl
- old plate with a slightly raised lip
- drill (or hammer and nail)
- potting mix

Wash the bowl thoroughly. Drill four to five holes in the base (alternatively use a nail and hammer to pierce bowl carefully). Sit on top of plate to catch excess dirt and water. Fill the bowl three-quarters full with soil. Plant seeds in sections of the bowl. Water generously and place in the sun until seedlings sprout. Once the garden begins to grow, encourage the kids to pick salad leaves for dinner.

MAKE STOCKING HEADS

- 2 tablespoons chive seeds or grass seeds
- nylon stocking foot
- 2–3 handfuls potting mix
- small glass jar
- water
- 2 googly eyes
- permanent marker
- double-sided tape

Spoon the seed into the stocking foot. Pour spoonfuls of the potting mix on top of the seed. Tie a knot in the stocking, leaving the excess fabric hanging. Fill a glass jar halfway with water and place the stocking head on top with the nylon tail in the water to serve as a wick. Attach googly eyes to the head and draw on a mouth with permanent marker. Set on a windowsill with sunlight. Be sure to check the water level in the jar every day, keeping it at least half full.

5. Get the kids cooking

The more involved the kids are, the more they'll learn to recognise foods and appreciate the benefits of healthy choices. And when they cook it themselves, the more likely they are to want to eat it!

Check out these studies:

- A study by City University London found that cooking classes aimed at both school pupils and adults had a positive impact on eating habits, with more pupils saying they ate more fruit and veg following the sessions.

- Another study, carried out by the School Food Trust in the UK, which measured the impact of a national network of school-based cooking clubs for 4–8 year olds, found that learning to cook improved their recognition and understanding of healthier foods – and their desire to eat them.

TOP TIPS TO GET THE KIDS COOKING

1. **Let them bake!** Get your kids pouring ingredients into the bowl. Teach them how to weigh ingredients or measure 1 teaspoon and get them kneading dough or mixing batter.

2. **Let them peel and chop.** Get the kids to scrub potatoes and Brussels sprouts for Sunday lunch. Or dry the rinsed lettuce with the salad spinner. Kids love to help, and you're developing their motor skills at the same time. When they're old enough, get them peeling and chopping veggies (with supervision).

3. **Let them do the fun stuff.** For the young ones (ages 2 and up) simple actions like pressing the button on the food processor or licking the bowl are exciting enough to get them thoroughly invested in the meal.

4. **Ask the kids to taste test.** Making them part of the process will get them more excited about eating the final product. Better yet, ask for their feedback. 'Do you love the saltiness?' 'How squishy is that dough!' You get the gist.

5. **Have the kids around when you're cooking.** If you don't have stacks of time to plan activities, just have the kids close by. Pop them on your hip when you're stirring the pot of sauce. As long as children are witnessing your actions they'll be absorbing them.

6. **Give them loads of positive feedback.** Always praise their efforts – even when mistakes are made.

Mum's THE WORD

Go DIY.
Make up your own 'packet mixes' for quick and easy baking. Place dry ingredients into a ziplock bag. Write instructions on the front in permanent marker. For example 'add 2 eggs, 125 ml milk, stir and pour into moulds'. Have a bunch set aside for rainy days or when kids have friends over. They'll love the simplicity and the reward of doing it all by themselves.

RECIPES

NAVIGATING THE RECIPES

The recipes in this book are mostly gluten free. They're also paleo and vegan friendly, easily adaptable to your family's style.

Throughout the book you'll see these icons to help you navigate the recipes:

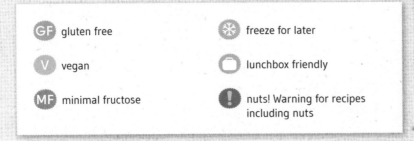

GF gluten free

V vegan

MF minimal fructose

❄ freeze for later

◻ lunchbox friendly

❗ nuts! Warning for recipes including nuts

A note on nuts

Many of the recipes in this book include nuts (nut butters, flours and meals). However, we're aware that schools are pretty much nut-free zones these days, so we've also included a handy warning icon on all the recipes with any kind of nut product, so you'll know which recipes you shouldn't send to school. And if you have a child with a nut allergy, these are the recipes to avoid.

A note on allergies

We take the risk of allergies very seriously, so we've created a helpful allergy substitution guide. You can find it on page 7.

A note on sweeteners

Rice malt syrup: This is a blend of maltose and glucose made from fermented, cooked rice. You can use this in place of sugar or honey in recipes, roughly in a 1:1 ratio. Some folk say it is less sweet than honey and sugar. We beg to differ and tend to put less of it in our recipes than many others would. You can find it in health-food shops and many supermarkets (in the baking section) and it costs about the same as honey. Look for brands that list organic rice as the only ingredient.

Stevia: This is a natural sweetener, derived from a leaf similar to mint and is composed of stevioside (which is 300 times sweeter than sugar) and rebaudioside (450 times sweeter than sugar). Stevia comes as a liquid or mixed with erythritol to form a granule, the latter version is readily available in many supermarkets (in the baking section). Look for granulated forms. When we refer to stevia in this book, we mean the granulated form. Most stevia granules can be used as you would sugar, although we tend to use about a third less.

Another thing to keep in mind: stevia can be bitter if used in excess so we tend to recommend rice malt syrup for kids.

Other sweeteners that are okay to use in moderation are xylitol (a sugar alcohol that can be digested by our bodies) and dextrose (100 per cent glucose). However we tend to avoid both as rice malt syrup breaks down as a complex carbohydrate thus releasing glucose into the body slowly.

The rest: Don't touch – most have been shown to be either carcinogenic or entirely indigestible, thus causing a myriad of health issues. Not good for the kids. Many of the fake sugars available are banned in parts of Europe, deemed unsafe. 'Nuf said.

Also stay clear of natural fructose like coconut nectar and agave. Both are equally as potent in their forms and will cause insulin spikes, which is what we're trying to avoid.

BEWARE

This is not a licence to go crazy on glucose.

Even non-fructose sugars, such as glucose, are not good to eat in large quantities and will cause insulin wobbliness too, albeit in a far more manageable way. What's more, studies at the University of Washington have found that consuming any kind of sweetener – even the 'fake' ones that don't contain sugar as such – can cause a blood sugar spike and continue a sugar addiction. Just the sweet taste can trigger insulin and metabolic responses.

A note on spices

There aren't too many kids we know who are big on chilli or other spices. But that doesn't mean you have to rule out flavoursome eating completely.

Try some mild curries with ingredients like tamarind, turmeric, cumin, coriander, cinnamon, cloves, coconut and curry leaves. They're gentle enough for developing palates.

Make your own marinades with ginger, lime juice, tamari, cashew nuts, sesame seeds, black pepper, garlic, coriander and mint. For the adventurous kid, add a sprinkle of chilli. The longer, fresh ones are generally milder.

Spice it up.
Adding warm spices like cinnamon, allspice and ginger creates the illusion of sweetness when baking.

CONTRIBUTORS

In addition to our recipes, this book features a bunch developed by I Quit Sugar readers.

Thank you to the 100+ of you who submitted recipes for this project. It's wonderful to see so much I Quit Sugar foodie action happening around the globe.

Some of our foodie and blogging friends also kicked in their creations. Thank you to:

Sha Ragnauth – creator and author of *Sugar Free Kids*, a site where Sha dedicates her time to creating sugar-free kids' recipes.

Kate Burbidge – a registered psychologist who is also a health nut in the kitchen. Kate is committed to ending people's dysfunctional relationships with food. Check out her site TheHealthyPsychologist.com.

Bree Hateley – creator of stokeswap.com.au, a website dedicated to providing healthy and wholesome tips for feeding kids.

Ruby Gallery – a mum dedicated to sharing her favourite paleo recipes, tried and tested on her two young boys. Her website paleoforkids.com.au includes recipe updates and tips especially for paleo followers.

Lee Holmes – author of multiple cookbooks including, *Supercharged Food: Eat Yourself Beautiful*. Lee blogs at SuperchargedFood.com.

Alice Nicholls – works with women, helping them connect their heart, mind and body using practical health and wellness information. She's also a gun in the kitchen! You can find her sugar-free offerings at TheWholeDaily.com.au.

Kasia Froncek

Hannah and Kate – who share their love of nutrition, exercise and food at thewholesomelife.tumblr.com.

Kira Westwick

Di Health

Corinna Rhodes

Milena Zanetti

Sophie Peters

Georgia Harding – blogs at wellnourished.com.au.

Natalie Bourke – is an Accredited Practising Dietitian and I Quit Sugar's community management guru. Check out her site www.healthbywholefoods.com.au.

SIMPLE STAPLES THAT GET KIDS TO THE TABLE

We've gathered a bunch of store-cupboard staples and reworked them to be sugar free and healthy enough for the kids to drench their greens in.

HOMEMADE TOMATO SAUCE

Tomato sauce is one of the biggest culprits when it comes to hidden sugars. In some cases it's 50 per cent sugar! Try this Homemade Tomato Sauce for a flavoursome yet familiar version of something every kid loves.

MAKES 500 ml

PREPARATION TIME
5 minutes

COOKING TIME
55 minutes

2 × 440 g cans whole peeled tomatoes (or 675 ml passata)

½ onion, chopped

⅓ cup (75 ml) apple cider vinegar

4 teaspoons rice malt syrup (or 2 teaspoons granulated stevia)

1 teaspoon ground allspice

1 teaspoon ground cinnamon

1 teaspoon ground cloves

1 teaspoon cayenne pepper

salt and freshly ground black pepper, to taste

1. Bring all the ingredients to the boil in a saucepan, crush the tomatoes with the back of a spoon then stir to distribute the spices. Reduce the heat and simmer for about 50 minutes or until the sauce reduces by almost half and is quite thick.

2. Blend with a hand-held blender or in a food processor. If the sauce is still a bit runny, return it to the heat and reduce for a little longer.

3. Divide the mixture into 2 × 250 ml sterilised glass jars and store in the fridge for up to one month.

> **TRICKY TIP**
>
> You can also make this in a slow cooker. Cook all the ingredients on high for 2–2½ hours. After blending, you might want to return it to the cooker for another 30 minutes, without the lid, to thicken it.

BBQ SAUCE

MAKES 250 ml

PREPARATION TIME
5 minutes

1 cup (250 ml) Homemade Tomato Sauce (see above)

2 tablespoons apple cider vinegar

2 tablespoons chilli powder

1 clove garlic, crushed

1 tablespoon paprika

1 teaspoon Tabasco sauce

1. Mix all the ingredients and store in a sterilised glass jar in the fridge for up to one month.

DECEPTIVELY SWEET CHILLI SAUCE

The standard stuff you buy in a bottle is pretty much caramel topping with a kick. The IQS way is to use a sugar-free thickener instead to achieve the sticky sauce-like consistency.

MAKES 300 ml

PREPARATION TIME
5 minutes

COOKING TIME
10 minutes

½ cup (125 ml) rice vinegar or apple cider vinegar

1 tablespoon rice malt syrup

1 red chilli (add extra for adults) or 2 teaspoons crushed dried chilli

140 ml water

4 tablespoons fish sauce

3 garlic cloves

½ teaspoon salt

1 tablespoon cornflour or arrowroot

1. Puree the vinegar, rice malt syrup, chilli, 100 ml of the water, fish sauce, garlic and salt in a blender, or finely chop the chilli and garlic first then combine with the rest of the ingredients in a jar, shaking vigorously.

2. Pour the mixture into a saucepan and bring to the boil over high heat. Reduce the heat to medium and simmer for 5–10 minutes, until reduced by about half.

3. Meanwhile, combine the cornflour or arrowroot and remaining water to make a thick paste. Whisk the paste into the sauce and simmer for 1 minute more.

4. Cool and store in a sterilised glass jar in the fridge for up to 2 weeks.

SATAY SAUCE

This is a tasty dipping sauce and works well drizzled over stir-fries or crunchy Asian salads.

MAKES 2 cups (500 ml)

PREPARATION TIME
5 minutes

COOKING TIME
10 minutes

1 × 400 ml can coconut cream

½ cup (115 g) natural, sugar-free and salt-free crunchy peanut butter

1 teaspoon ground turmeric

1 teaspoon ground ginger

1 teaspoon ground coriander

pinch of ground cumin

½ teaspoon sea salt

1. Combine all the ingredients in a small saucepan and bring to the boil over medium heat, stirring constantly.

2. Reduce the heat to low and cook for 10 minutes, stirring occasionally, for the sauce to cook down and thicken.

3. Transfer to a sterilised glass jar and store in the fridge for up to 2 weeks.

HOMEMADE SPRINKLES

Recipe by Kasia Froncek
*What's a birthday cake without some sprinkles? This recipe is a great substitute
for those sugary speckles that kids love so much.*

MAKES ½ cup
(125 ml)

PREPARATION TIME
5 minutes
(+ overnight
drying)

**A Dash of Colour
(see page 133)**

½ cup (115 g) dextrose

1 egg white

1. Line a baking tray with baking paper.

2. Add A Dash of Colour to the dextrose and 'rub in' with the back of a spoon.

3. Once the colour starts to mix in, gradually add the egg white, about a teaspoon
    at a time and add more colour to get the desired shade.

4. Mix until well combined and smooth, the consistency should be thick but also
    slightly runny.

5. Spoon the mixture into a ziplock bag, seal the top and cut a tiny corner off.
    Squeeze out the icing in thin long lines.

6. Leave overnight to set and dry. Break up into smaller 'sprinkle' sized pieces
    with your fingers. Store sprinkles in an airtight container for up to 2 weeks.

> **TRICKY TIP**
>
> Serve on top of cakes, or sprinkle over Simple Coconut Ice Cream
> (see page 131).

KIDS' BERRY JAM

MAKES ¾ cup
(175 ml)

PREPARATION TIME
5 minutes

COOKING TIME
5 minutes

**1 cup (125 g) blueberries or
strawberries (frozen or fresh)**

4 tablespoons chia seeds or arrowroot

1 tablespoon rice malt syrup

1 tablespoon water

1. Blend all ingredients in a blender until smooth.

2. Pour into a saucepan and heat over medium heat until the mixture begins
    to bubble.

3. Reduce the heat and whisk constantly until thickened, about 3–5 minutes.
    Pour into a hot sterilised jar and cool. Once open, store in the fridge for up
    to 5 days.

KIDS' BERRY JAM

SUGAR-FREE NUT-ELLA

SUGAR-FREE NUT-ELLA

This version will fool even the most sceptical child. It's great on a slice of toast or a few rice cakes for afternoon tea. For a decadent treat use it as a sauce for the Chocolate Lava Brownies (see page 72).

MAKES 1 cup
(250 ml)

PREPARATION TIME
5 minutes

COOKING TIME
10 minutes

1 cup (135 g) hazelnuts

½ cup (125 ml) coconut milk

1 tablespoon rice malt syrup

1 tablespoon macadamia oil

4 tablespoons raw cacao powder

1 tablespoon vanilla powder

1. Preheat the oven to 180°C (gas 4). Line a baking tray with baking paper.

2. Bake the hazelnuts on the tray for 8–10 minutes or until browned and fragrant. Rub off most of the skins as they can be bitter (you don't have to be too precise).

3. Grind the nuts in a food processor until smooth. Add the remaining ingredients and process until well mixed. Store in a sterilised glass jar in the fridge for up to 1 month.

> **TRICKY TIP**
>
> For more of a 'saucy' consistency add extra coconut milk when blending.

PUMPKIN PUREE

We always have a stash of this stuff in the freezer, saved in ½ cup (125 ml) portions and in ice-cube trays.

MAKES 2–3 cups
(500–750 ml)

PREPARATION TIME
5 minutes

COOKING TIME
1 hour

1 large pumpkin, cut into 4 big wedges

2 tablespoons olive oil

pinch of sea salt

1. Preheat the oven to 175°C (gas 3). Scoop out and discard the pumpkin seeds and pulp. Put the pumpkin wedges on a baking tray, and then rub with the olive oil and salt.

2. Bake on the middle rack until tender – about 1 hour. (If you're pressed for time, cut the pumpkin into smaller chunks and bake for 30 minutes.)

3. Scoop out the flesh and puree using a hand-held blender or mash well with a potato masher.

4. Once cool, if not using immediately, store in batches in the freezer for up to 1 month.

ICE MAGIC

This recipe has all the magic that the real stuff has minus the overload of sugar. Simply pour it over the Simple Coconut Ice Cream (see page 131) and watch it set hard before your child's eyes!

MAKES 1¼ cups (300 ml)

PREPARATION TIME
5 minutes

COOKING TIME
5 minutes

½ cup (100 g) coconut oil

½ cup (50 g) raw cacao powder

½ teaspoon granulated stevia, or to taste

¼ teaspoon sea salt

1. Melt the coconut oil in a small saucepan over low heat then add the remaining ingredients, whisking well until the stevia is dissolved.

2. Allow to cool slightly, and then pour over Simple Coconut Ice Cream (see page 131).

> **TRICKY TIP**
>
> To store, pour any leftover mixture into a covered container in the fridge and melt in the microwave for 30 seconds when you need to use it.

WHIPPED COCONUT CREAM

With just two ingredients this has to be the simplest accompaniment to serve with a slice of sugar-free cake.

MAKES 1¼ cups (300 ml)

PREPARATION TIME
overnight

1 × 400 ml can coconut cream

1 tablespoon granulated stevia

1. Place the can of coconut cream upside down in the fridge overnight (be sure not to shake it beforehand).

2. The next day, turn it right way up and open the can without shaking it.

3. Spoon out the top layer of liquid (keep this for smoothies or other recipes requiring coconut milk or coconut water).

4. Leave the rest of the harder cream in the can, add the stevia, and then blend using a hand-held blender until thick and creamy.

> **TRICKY TIP**
>
> If you don't have a hand-held blender, remove the cream from the can and whip using a hand mixer or in a blender.

ICE MAGIC

MUSHY PEA MASH

MAKES 2 cups
(500 ml)

PREPARATION TIME
5 minutes

COOKING TIME
15 minutes

2 potatoes, peeled

2 cups (350 g) broccoli florets

1 cup (150 g) frozen peas

5 mint leaves, finely chopped

2 tablespoons olive oil or butter

sea salt and freshly ground black pepper, to taste

1. Cut the potatoes into quarters, place them in a saucepan and cover with cold water. Bring to the boil over high heat, then reduce to a rolling simmer and cook for about 10 minutes, or until the potatoes are tender.

2. Add the broccoli and peas and cook for another 3–5 minutes, until cooked.

3. Drain the vegetables and pour into a bowl. Add the mint and oil or butter.

4. Season with salt and pepper and blitz with a hand-held blender or in a food processor to your preferred consistency.

> **TRICKY TIP**
>
> **Mix up the consistency.** For the younger kids, blitz into a puree. Leave chunky for the older kids so they can dollop it onto their dinner.

CAULI-CREAM CHEESE SAUCE

This is a winner with the kids; an easy accompaniment with most dishes plus it's packed with hidden vegetables.

MAKES 1½ cups
(350 ml)

PREPARATION TIME
5 minutes

COOKING TIME
15 minutes

½ cauliflower, broken into small florets

½ cup (125 ml) cream

40 g butter

⅓ cup (40 g) grated cheddar cheese

sea salt, to taste

1. Steam the cauliflower until just cooked through, about 8 minutes.

2. Combine the cauliflower, cream and butter in a saucepan, season with salt, then cover and cook over low heat for 10 minutes until soft.

3. Blend until smooth using a hand-held blender or mash with a potato masher.

4. Stir in grated cheese until melted.

BREAKFAST FOR BRAIN POWER

This chapter is brimful of tote-able and fun breakfast ideas to replace those sugar-laden 'healthy' cereals.

PUMPKIN PIKELETS

*Serve up these simple pikelets with grated apple, walnuts, extra cinnamon,
and a drizzle of rice malt syrup, or with a spoon of Kids' Berry Jam (see page 20).*

MAKES 6

PREPARATION TIME

5 minutes

COOKING TIME

15 minutes

½ cup (125 ml) Pumpkin Puree (see page 23)

1 tablespoon coconut flour

½ teaspoon ground cinnamon

2 eggs

butter or coconut oil, for cooking

1. Combine the Pumpkin Puree, flour, cinnamon and eggs in a small bowl.

2. Heat a little butter or oil in a small frying pan over medium heat and drop in 2-tablespoon dollops of the pikelet mixture.

3. Cook for 3 minutes on each side, or until golden.

FLOWER POWER EGGS

*For a pop of colour, try this recipe with orange, yellow and green peppers.
The kids will love it.*

MAKES 4

PREPARATION TIME

3 minutes

COOKING TIME

5 minutes

coconut oil, butter or ghee, for cooking

1 red, green or orange pepper, or a mixture

4 eggs

1. Cut the pepper in four 1.5-cm thick rings and place in a lightly oiled frying pan over low heat.

2. Crack an egg into the middle of each ring, then cover and cook for 3–5 minutes until cooked through.

3. If you like your yolks firm, break the yolks and then cover and cook over low heat until both whites and yolks are firm.

> **TRICKY TIP**
>
> Use the leftover pepper in a soup, salad, juice or casserole.

FLOWER POWER EGGS

FACE PLANT PANCAKES

This is the perfect dish to get fussy children excited about food. Making their pancakes a visual feast is the best way to grab their imagination!

MAKES 15

PREPARATION TIME
5 minutes

COOKING TIME
40 minutes

1 large beetroot

2 eggs

1 cup (250 ml) yoghurt

½ cup (125 ml) milk

3 tablespoons coconut oil

½ teaspoon vanilla powder

1 tablespoon rice malt syrup

1½ cups (185 g) gluten-free flour

2 teaspoons baking powder

1 teaspoon bicarbonate of soda

4 tablespoons chia seeds

¼ teaspoon salt

butter or coconut oil, for cooking

fruit, to serve

cream cheese, yoghurt or Whipped Coconut Cream (see page 24), to serve

1. Preheat the oven to 180°C (gas 4).

2. Wrap the beetroot in foil and place on a baking tray. Bake for 30 minutes until soft when pierced. Peel off the skin and blend with a hand-held blender. You will need ½ cup (125 ml) puree for the pancakes.

3. Beat the eggs, yoghurt, milk, oil, vanilla, beetroot puree and rice malt syrup until combined.

4. Sift the flour, baking powder and bicarbonate of soda on top of the wet ingredients.

5. Add the chia seeds and salt and mix until combined.

6. Heat a little butter or oil in a frying pan over medium heat and pour in ¼-cup (60 ml) dollops of the mixture. Cook for about 2 minutes until bubbles break through. Turn carefully and cook for an additional 1–2 minutes, until lightly browned and cooked through. Depending on the size of the pan, you will probably need to cook in batches.

7. Serve with blueberry 'eyes', an apple slice 'mouth' and a cream cheese, yoghurt or Whipped Coconut Cream 'splodged nose'.

CHOC AVO
BREKKIE SMASH

This smash is healthy enough for breakfast – easily transportable and it'll keep the kids going until lunchtime. Why not make up a jar for yourself?

MAKES 4–6

PREPARATION TIME
15 minutes
(+ 1 hour setting)

2 ripe avocados, halved and deseeded

½ cup (125 ml) coconut cream, chilled

4 tablespoons raw cacao powder

1 tablespoon chia seeds

2 teaspoons rice malt syrup

1 teaspoon vanilla extract or
a sprinkle of vanilla powder

½ teaspoon ground cinnamon

salt, to taste

1½ cups (175 g) frozen berries

1½ teaspoons granulated stevia

¾ cup (60 g) shredded coconut or
rolled oats

1. Blend the avocado, coconut cream, raw cacao, chia seeds, rice malt syrup, vanilla, cinnamon and salt in a blender until smooth. Scrape the mixture into a bowl, cover and chill the mixture in the fridge for at least 1 hour to set.

2. While the mousse mixture is setting, pulse the frozen berries and stevia in a blender to form a chunky puree. Stop before the mixture is too smooth.

3. Line up 4–6 sterilised jars or glasses. Spoon 4 tablespoons of the mousse mixture into the base of each jar. Spoon a layer of berry puree over the top and then a layer of shredded coconut or rolled oats. Repeat the process until the jars are full.

4. Serve immediately or seal and leave in the fridge for up to 2 days.

Go easy on the chocolate.
Use less cacao for young children who might not have the palate for it yet.

PEANUT BUTTER 'N' JELLY WHIP

This recipe calls for you to soak the oats. Having the husks softened means the meal will be gentler on tiny tums.

MAKES 2

PREPARATION TIME
10 minutes
(+ overnight
soaking)

½ cup (50 g) rolled oats

2 tablespoons protein powder

1 tablespoon chia seeds

1 teaspoon vanilla extract or
¼ teaspoon vanilla powder

1½ cups (375 ml) milk (any kind)

1 tablespoon coconut flakes

1 tablespoon Kids' Berry Jam
(see page 20)

1 tablespoon peanut butter
(or almond butter)

walnuts or pecans, to serve

1. Blitz the oats, protein powder, chia seeds, vanilla and milk in a blender until smooth. Pour into two jars and top with coconut flakes. Leave to soak overnight in the fridge, lids on.

2. The next day top the porridge mixture with the jam, a dollop of peanut butter and some walnuts or pecans.

> **TRICKY TIP**
> During the cooler months warm the mixture in the microwave before serving.

BUGS BUNNY CRUMBLE PUDDING

Mums and dads don't be fooled. This one's a winner for you guys as well!

SERVES 4

PREPARATION TIME
15 minutes

COOKING TIME
50 minutes

CARROT CRUMBLE

5 tablespoons coconut oil

2 carrots, grated

4 tablespoons linseeds (optional)

½ teaspoon ground cloves

1 teaspoon cinnamon

⅔ cup (65 g) rolled oats

⅓ cup (20 g) coconut flakes

⅓ cup (40 g) almonds, chopped

4 tablespoons pumpkin seeds

4 tablespoons rice malt syrup

1 orange, zested and juiced, and extra zest to serve

CHIA PUDDING

1 × 420 ml can coconut milk

2 tablespoons rice malt syrup

1½ teaspoons ground cinnamon

4 tablespoons chia seeds

1. Preheat the oven to 180°C (gas 4).

2. Place all the chia pudding ingredients, except the chia seeds in a saucepan over low heat and slowly bring to the boil, stirring occasionally. Remove from the heat and set aside to cool. Stir in the chia seeds for about 15 minutes until thickened and pour into individual glasses or a pudding dish.

3. For the carrot crumble, melt the coconut oil in a frying pan over medium heat. Add the carrot, linseeds (if using) and spices, and cook, stirring constantly for 4–5 minutes or until fragrant.

4. Add the remaining ingredients and cook for about 10 minutes, until soft. Remove from the heat and spread the mixture over a baking tray. Bake for about 20 minutes, tossing after 10 minutes, or until it resembles a crumb mixture.

5. Sprinkle the crumble on top of the chia pudding and grate the extra orange zest over the pudding to serve.

Mum's THE WORD

Add some texture.
Use chia seeds like sprinkles, they add a nice crunch to recipes!

UP AND AT 'EM BREAKFAST WHIP

Don't waste money on chemical-laden, preservative-packed poppers. Make your own grab-and-go brekky instead. You can prepare this the night before for convenience.

MAKES 1

PREPARATION TIME
2 minutes

2–3 Weetabix (or any low-sugar wheat breakfast biscuit), crushed

⅓ cup (75 ml) milk (any kind)

2 ice cubes

1 tablespoon almond butter or protein powder

2 frozen or fresh strawberries (optional)

2 teaspoons rice malt syrup (optional)

full-fat, natural yoghurt and walnuts (optional), to serve

1. Place all the ingredients, except for the yoghurt and walnuts, into a blender and blend until smooth.

2. Pour into a jar or glass and top with yoghurt and walnuts, if you like.

SUGAR-FREE CACAO POPS

Recipe by Bree Hateley

MAKES 5 cups
(150 g)

PREPARATION TIME
10 minutes
(+ cooling and
setting time)

COOKING TIME
5 minutes

1 cup (200 g) coconut oil

½ (120 g) cup cacao butter

4 tablespoons rice malt syrup

4 tablespoons raw cacao powder

pinch of sea salt

½ teaspoon vanilla powder or vanilla essence (optional)

4 tablespoons desiccated coconut

5 cups (150 g) brown puffed rice, puffed quinoa, amaranth, buckwheat or a mixture of all four

milk (any kind) and berries, to serve

1. Line a tray with baking paper.

2. Combine the coconut oil, cacao butter, rice malt syrup, cacao powder, sea salt and vanilla in a medium saucepan over low heat and cook, stirring until melted and combined. Stir in the coconut, remove from the heat and set aside to cool slightly.

3. Pour the mixture over the dry grains in a large bowl and stir well.

4. Spread the mixture over the prepared tray and set aside. Store in an airtight container in the fridge for up to 1 week.

5. Serve with milk and a handful of berries.

UP AND AT 'EM BREAKFAST WHIP

CLASSIC FRENCH TOAST

SERVES 1

PREPARATION TIME
5 minutes

COOKING TIME
5 minutes

1 teaspoon butter

2 eggs, whisked

4 tablespoons milk

¼ teaspoon vanilla powder

pinch of ground cinnamon

pinch of granulated stevia (optional)

2 slices good quality sourdough or gluten-free bread

baked peaches (or fresh if you prefer), to serve

natural yoghurt, to serve

1. Melt the butter in a frying pan over medium–high heat.

2. Combine the eggs, milk, vanilla, cinnamon and stevia in a shallow dish. Dip the slices of bread into the mixture until coated. Let excess drip away. Add the eggy bread slices to the pan.

3. Cook for 1–2 minutes each side, until golden and crisp. Transfer to a plate and serve with baked peaches and yoghurt.

TRICKY TIP

A quick and easy way to cook peaches is to preheat the oven to 200°C (gas 6). Toss sliced peaches in ½ teaspoon of melted rice malt syrup and 1 teaspoon of lemon juice. Bake for 20 minutes until tender. Yum!

VARIATIONS

Vegan

Replace the milk and eggs with a 165 ml can of coconut milk and 1 tablespoon of chia seeds. Use coconut oil instead of butter. Top slices with toasted coconut flakes and a drizzle of almond butter.

Pumpkin

Remove one egg from the recipe, and combine ½ cup (125 ml) pureed steamed pumpkin with the remaining egg. Add ¼ teaspoon ground cinnamon and freshly grated nutmeg to the mixture. Serve with rice malt syrup and chopped nuts.

Raspberry and Ricotta

Mash ½ cup (60 g) raspberries with ½ cup (120 g) fresh ricotta and serve with the French toast.

Savoury chives

Omit the vanilla, cinnamon, stevia and toppings from the recipe. Add 2 tablespoons finely chopped chives, 4 tablespoons grated parmesan, salt and pepper to the egg mixture. Serve with wilted spinach and fresh avocado.

WHEN A VEGGIE IS NOT A VEGGIE

*Tricked-up recipes and useful tips
for getting as much dense nutrition
into your little ones as possible
(without them knowing)!*

HOW TO GET YOUR KIDS EATING GREENS

You'll notice we harp on about dense nutrition – it really is a key factor in staving off cravings.

Try these clever tips to get more greens into your kids:

- **Add spinach to smoothies with berries.** The berries will mask the colour and flavour of the spinach.
- **Make a batch of green guacamole.** Serve with tacos or chicken. Use one avocado, a good squeeze of lemon, half a finely diced tomato and season with some salt and pepper. Add some toasted tortillas to serve.
- **Camouflage with purees.** Puree peas, pumpkin and carrot until smooth and fold through mash potato for a lighter version of a household favourite.
- **Bulk with broccoli.** Add lightly steamed chopped broccoli florets to scrambled eggs for some texture and green goodness.
- **Try coco-nutty cabbage.** Wilt shredded green cabbage down in a pan with coconut oil. Stir through 4 tablespoons of desiccated coconut until lightly toasted. The sweetness and crunchy texture will mask the cabbage-y flavour.
- **Layer spinach in lasagne.** Wilt down 3 cups (150 g) of spinach in butter or coconut oil and layer between sheets of pasta in a lasagne.
- **Make bacon Brussels sprouts.** Roast one rasher bacon, chopped, in a pan with 1 cup (115 g) Brussels sprouts, cut into quarters, or 1 cup (100 g) cabbage, cut into 3-cm thick wedges, in a 200°C (gas 6) oven for 30 minutes, stirring a few times. Serve with a splash of apple cider vinegar.
- **Make green spaghetti.** Using a regular peeler or a fancy ribboning tool peel courgettes to resemble spaghetti and stir through a low-sugar pasta sauce with a dollop of ricotta cheese on top.
- **Puree and freeze pesto.** This is a great timesaver and an easy way to inject healthy flavour into any meal. Simply make your pesto of choice and freeze in ice trays. Pop out a few cubes and stir through pasta or quinoa.

The best way to cook greens:

Steaming is our preferred method, always served with some olive, coconut or macadamia oil, or a generous knob of butter. A double steamer works best, otherwise use a bamboo steamer atop a saucepan, or a mesh steamer placed in a saucepan. Layer the vegetables, placing the longest-to-cook (and stalks) at the bottom first, then adding those that only need a quick heat through (leaves) on top. Any vegetables that need to be boiled (such as frozen peas) can be done underneath (in the saucepan of water) at the same time.

Let the cat out of the bag!
Once your kids have tried a recipe with hidden veggies a few times, let them know what you've been up to! Explain that the reason it tastes so good is because the carrot made it sweet or the beetroot added colour.

DID YOU KNOW?

Vegetables should always be eaten with fat.
Many of the important vitamins in vegetables –
A, E, K and D – are fat-soluble only. Add some
avo to your salads, and olive oil or butter to your
veggies just like your grandmother used to.
Your kids aren't absorbing the maximum nutrients
if you don't.

FLUFFY CARROT MOUSSE

Make this satisfying mousse in a big ol' baking dish or dollop into individual ramekins for afternoon snacks.

SERVES 4

PREPARATION TIME
5 minutes

COOKING TIME
1 hour 20 minutes

coconut oil, butter or ghee, for greasing

5–6 cups (750–900 g) chopped carrot

4 tablespoons almond meal

3 eggs

1 tablespoon rice malt syrup

½ teaspoon ground nutmeg

½ teaspoon ground cinnamon

1 tablespoon grated orange zest

1. Preheat the oven to 180°C (gas 4). Lightly grease a small baking dish.

2. Steam the carrots for 15–20 minutes until soft. Transfer to a blender and blend with the remaining ingredients until smooth.

3. Pour the lot into the baking dish and bake for 1 hour until browned around the edges and cooked in the centre.

4. Serve warm straight from the oven or allow to cool and then refrigerate.

Introduce your kids to new foods during growth spurts. They're more receptive when their bodies are craving food.

CHEESY GREEN FRITTERS

MAKES 8–10

PREPARATION TIME
10 minutes

COOKING TIME
10 minutes

2–3 large courgettes

1 tablespoon coconut flour

3 eggs

2 tablespoons ricotta

2 tablespoons crumbled feta

1 teaspoon coconut oil

salt and freshly ground black pepper, to taste

cream cheese, softened, to serve

1. Grate the courgettes using a food processor with a shredding disc or a box grater. You will need 2 cups (500 ml).

2. Sift the coconut flour into the eggs in a bowl and beat them together with a fork until smooth.

3. Add the courgettes, ricotta, feta, salt and pepper and mix thoroughly.

4. Heat the oil in a frying pan over medium heat and spoon in dollops of batter.

5. Cook for 2 minutes on each side until golden.

6. Serve warm with cream cheese dolloped on top.

SHREK BREAD

Recipe by Hannah and Kate at thewholesomelife.tumblr.com

Pack this bread with as many greens as you can find in the fridge; it's a great way to use up all those veggies that are on the edge of going bad. To serve, toast a slice and spread with some raw nut butter for an afternoon snack.

MAKES 1 loaf

PREPARATION TIME
10 minutes

COOKING TIME
25 minutes

coconut oil, butter or ghee, for greasing

3 cups (180 g) mixed greens (for example: 1 cup (60 g) each of baby spinach, kale and Swiss chard)

1 cup (100 g) almond meal

½ cup (60 g) sunflower seeds

4 tablespoons flaxmeal or LSA

2 teaspoons baking powder

¼ teaspoon sea salt

2 eggs

4 tablespoons melted coconut oil

1. Preheat the oven to 200°C (gas 6) and grease a small loaf tin (8 cm × 20 cm). Blitz all the greens in a blender or food processor on high speed until finely broken down.

2. Add all the dry ingredients to the processed greens and blend on medium–low speed until well combined.

3. Add the eggs and coconut oil to the blender and blend on medium speed until well incorporated.

4. Spoon the mixture into the prepared tin; it should fill just over halfway. Bake for about 25 minutes or until a skewer comes out clean when inserted into the middle of the loaf.

5. Turn onto a wire rack to cool before slicing. Store in an airtight container; this will keep for a couple of days but is best eaten on the day it's baked.

DID YOU KNOW?

Spinach is a superfood.

Spinach has more than twice as much protein and fibre, five times more iron, eight times more magnesium, seven times more Vitamin C, and 20 times more Vitamin A than lettuce. Pack it into as many meals as you can for a boost in nutrients.

HAM AND CHEESE CAULIFLOWER PIZZA

Cauliflower is such a versatile ingredient; you'll find it pops up quite a bit throughout this book. This recipe uses cauliflower as a base instead of regular pizza bases.

SERVES 4

PREPARATION TIME
15 minutes

COOKING TIME
45 minutes

BASE

1 cauliflower, grated (by hand or in a food processor until it's rice-sized, but not pulverised) and par-cooked (steamed or boiled), well drained, cooled slightly and water squeezed out

100 g goat's cheese or
1 cup (115 g) grated cheddar cheese

2 eggs

sea salt and freshly ground black pepper, to taste

TOPPING

⅓ cup (75 ml) Homemade Tomato Sauce (see page 18)

½ cup (60 g) grated cheddar cheese

100 g shaved ham

1. Preheat the oven to 200°C (gas 6). Line a baking tray with baking paper. To make the base, mix the cauliflower with the cheese and egg in a large bowl. Season with salt and pepper.

2. Using a wooden spoon or your hands, shape the mixture into 1 large pizza base or 4 small, directly on the prepared tray. The bases should be about 1–1½ cm thick. Bake for 30–35 minutes, or until firm and golden, then remove from the oven.

3. To make the topping, smear the Homemade Tomato Sauce over the base or bases. Sprinkle with half the cheese and then scatter the ham on top. Sprinkle with the remaining cheese.

4. Bake for a further 8–10 minutes, until the cheese has melted and serve warm.

Use this cauliflower base instead of regular pizza bases.
Mix and match ingredients depending on what you have in the fridge. If the kids are having a movie night make the bases in advance and freeze.

VEGGIE GARDEN POT PIES

Use veggies that the kids have grown in their garden (see page 10) to make this dish all the more satisfying.

MAKES 4

PREPARATION TIME
10 minutes

COOKING TIME
40 minutes

1 tablespoon olive oil

1 onion, finely chopped

2 red peppers, cut into 3 cm strips

4 courgettes, chopped into 3 cm pieces

300 g squash (any type), chopped into 3 cm pieces

½ × 400 g can chopped tomatoes

1 teaspoon dried thyme

½ cup (125 ml) vegetable or chicken stock

sea salt and freshly ground black pepper, to taste

3 tablespoons frozen peas

200 g potatoes (desiree works well)

20 g butter

⅓ cup (35 g) grated tasty cheese

1. Preheat the oven to 180°C (gas 4).

2. Heat the oil in a frying pan over a medium-high heat. Add the onion and cook, stirring occasionally, for 5 minutes or until soft.

3. Add the peppers, courgettes and squash to the pan and cook, stirring occasionally, for 7–8 minutes until the vegetables have softened.

4. Add the tomato, thyme and stock. Season with salt and pepper. Keep cooking for a further 5 minutes until the liquid has reduced and vegetables have collapsed into a stew. Take off the heat and stir the peas through.

5. Meanwhile place the potatoes in a large saucepan, cover with cold salted water, bring to the boil then simmer for 10–15 minutes until soft. Drain in a colander.

6. Mash the potato, butter and salt and pepper until smooth.

7. Divide the vegetable mixture into four ramekins or one baking dish. Spoon the mash on top of the vegetable mix and top with the cheese.

8. Bake the pies for 20 minutes, until cheese is melted and golden brown.

TRICKY TIP

For some extra protein add 150 g skinless salmon chunks to the pie just before baking.

DID YOU KNOW?

One of the best sources of Vitamin C is red pepper.
It has double the Vitamin C of an orange. Throw it into meals to maximise your kids' Vitamin C consumption.

MEATLESS MEATBALLS

Recipe by Kira Westwick

MAKES 24

PREPARATION TIME
10 minutes

COOKING TIME
20 minutes

5 carrots, finely grated

1 egg

180 g feta, crumbled

¼ onion, finely chopped

1 teaspoon each dried oregano, basil, thyme and garlic powder

2–3 teaspoons coconut flour

sea salt, to taste

olive or coconut oil, to drizzle

homemade tzatziki and salad or pasta with kale or broccoli pesto, to serve

1. Preheat the oven to 180°C (gas 4). Line a baking tray with baking paper.

2. Place the carrot and egg in a blender or food processor and pulse until slightly mushy. Transfer to a bowl, add the feta, onion and dried herbs and combine.

3. Gradually add 1 teaspoon at a time of coconut flour until you have a nice consistency for rolling balls. Alternatively use a food processor to bring everything together, pulsing to get the right consistency.

4. Roll the mixture into even tablespoon-sized balls and line up evenly spaced on the prepared tray. Drizzle with the olive or coconut oil and bake for 15–20 minutes or until golden and crisp on the outside, and soft in the middle.

5. Serve with homemade tzatziki and salad or alternatively toss through pasta with kale or broccoli pesto.

> **TRICKY TIP**
>
> If you can't source coconut flour you can use ⅓ cup (about 30 g) wholegrain breadcrumbs, almond meal, crushed macadamia nuts or walnuts.

SNEAKY GREEN CHOCO-NUT LOLLIES

Recipe by Kate Burbidge

This creamy chocolate icy pole has three layers and the sneaky addition of greens to keep the kiddies fuelled up and none the wiser.

MAKES 6

PREPARATION TIME
15 minutes
(+ freezing)

COCONUT LAYER

1 fresh young coconut

1 cup (250 ml) coconut water

1 tablespoon chia seeds

CHOCOLATE LAYER

1 avocado, halved and stoned

1 cup (50 g) baby spinach or kale

1 cup (250 ml) milk of choice (coconut, fresh almond milk, goat's or full-fat cow's milk will work)

1 heaped tablespoon raw cacao powder

2 teaspoons rice malt syrup

RASPBERRY LAYER

1 cup (125 g) fresh or defrosted raspberries

FIRST MAKE THE COCONUT LAYER

1. Crack open the coconut and use a spoon to scoop out the flesh.

2. Combine the coconut water, flesh and chia seeds in a blender and blend until thick.

3. Divide between six ice lolly moulds and pop into freezer until firm.

NEXT MAKE THE CHOCOLATE LAYER

1. Combine all the ingredients in a blender and blend until thick. This is a good time to check whether it is sweet enough for the little ones, add a little more rice malt syrup if required and blend again.

2. Spoon on top of the coconut layer and pop into freezer until firm.

FINALLY MAKE THE RASPBERRY LAYER

1. Using the back of a spoon, mash raspberries or blend until just combined but still chunky. Spoon on top of chocolate layer and pop into the freezer overnight.

SALT AND VINEGAR KALE CRISPS

SERVES 4

PREPARATION TIME
10 minutes

COOKING TIME
10 minutes

2 large bunches kale or cavolo nero, stalk removed

1½ tablespoons apple cider vinegar

2 tablespoons olive oil

good pinch of sea salt

1. Preheat the oven to 200°C (gas 6). Line two large baking trays with baking paper.

2. Tear the kale roughly into 4 cm squares.

3. Toss in a large bowl with the vinegar, oil and salt.

4. Lay the kale out evenly in a single layer on the trays and bake for 5–10 minutes until crisp.

5. Serve hot or cold for afternoon tea.

> ### TRICKY TIP
>
> Remove kale stalks as they're difficult to digest. To do this, hold the end of the stalk and run your fingers down, shearing the leaf off.

SAME-SAME
BUT DIFFERENT

Here, some kid classics with an IQS makeover.
They taste so naughty the kids will be convinced
they're wearing you down!

NOURISHING NACHOS

SERVES 4

PREPARATION TIME
5 minutes

COOKING TIME
7 minutes

4–6 pitta breads, cut into 'chips'

olive oil, to drizzle

2 tomatoes, chopped

1 × 400 g can red kidney beans, drained and well rinsed

1 small red onion, finely chopped

4 tablespoons mixed parsley and coriander leaves, finely chopped

2 teaspoons apple cider vinegar

1 avocado, halved and stoned

1 cup (110 g) crumbled feta

juice of 1 lemon

sea salt, to taste

1 cup (115 g) grated cheddar cheese

1. Preheat the grill. Place pitta 'chips' on a large tray in a single layer and drizzle lightly with olive oil. Grill for 3–4 minutes, turning halfway, or until lightly browned.

2. Mix the chopped tomato, beans, onion, herbs and apple cider vinegar in a bowl. Season with salt and set aside.

3. Mash the avocado, feta and lemon juice together in a separate bowl and sprinkle with a little salt.

4. Place a layer of the pitta chips on a large ovenproof plate or in a large casserole dish and lightly sprinkle with about half the cheddar cheese. Follow with the bean salsa mix and the remaining cheddar cheese.

5. Grill for about 3 minutes or until the cheese is melted and golden. Scoop onto plates and top with avocado and feta mixture.

CAULIFLOWER MAC AND CHEESE

This sneaky recipe is laden with hidden veggies and the kids won't have a clue they're eating something 'healthy' as they tuck in. For a crunchy golden topping, sprinkle some grated stale bread or breadcrumbs on top before placing in the oven.

SERVES 4

PREPARATION TIME
15 minutes

COOKING TIME
1 hour

1 cauliflower, cut into florets

½ cup (75 g) 3-cm cubed pumpkin or squash

olive oil, to sprinkle

2 teaspoons cumin seeds

60 g butter

½ cup (60 g) flour

2 thyme sprigs, leaves finely chopped

1½ cups (375 ml) milk

1 cup (250 ml) crème fraiche or sour cream

1 cup (115 g) finely grated cheddar cheese

1 cup (100 g) finely grated parmesan

1 cup (125 g) gluten-free penne (any variety of pasta will work)

1. Preheat the oven to 180°C (gas 4). Sprinkle the cauliflower and pumpkin with olive oil and cumin seeds and bake for about 15 minutes or until brown. Remove from oven and pull apart into smaller florets.

2. Melt the butter in a large saucepan, add the flour and thyme and whisk to a smooth paste. Slowly add the milk and crème fraiche over medium heat, whisking constantly until the mixture boils and thickens. Remove from the heat and stir in three quarters of each of the cheeses, saving some for the top layer.

3. Cook the pasta following packet instructions. Drain and rinse.

4. Combine the pasta, cauliflower, pumpkin and cheese sauce. Sprinkle the remaining cheese on top and bake for about 40 minutes or until golden brown and heated through.

BUTTERNUT
BAKED BEANS

Recipe by Hannah and Kate at thewholesomelife.tumblr.com

MAKES 6

PREPARATION TIME
10 minutes

COOKING TIME
40 minutes

½ butternut squash, peeled and diced

olive oil, for cooking

1 onion, finely diced

2 garlic cloves

1 teaspoon paprika

1 teaspoon mustard powder

1 teaspoon tamari

2 cups (400 g) cannellini or red kidney beans, soaked overnight and cooked (or 2 × 400 g cans of beans, drained and well rinsed)

small handful fresh herbs

sourdough toast, to serve

1. Preheat the oven to 160°C (gas 3).

2. Steam half of the diced squash until soft (save the other half if you would like squash chunks, but if you want it all to be smooth just steam the whole lot!).

3. Heat the oil in a frying pan over medium heat and cook the onion for 3–4 minutes or until lightly browned.

4. Blend the cooked onion, steamed squash, garlic, paprika, mustard and tamari in a food processor until smooth.

5. Combine the beans and the squash mixture (and the uncooked squash chunks if you have them) in a baking dish. Cover the baking dish with aluminium foil and bake for 30 minutes.

6. Serve on toast, sprinkled with fresh herbs.

PUMPKIN GINGER SPICE GRANOLA BARS

These are the perfect grab-and-go snack. Keep a few on you or in the car in a ziplock bag for when the kids are asking for a treat. This recipe contains ½ teaspoon of added sugar per serve so only enjoy it as an occasional treat.

MAKES 16

PREPARATION TIME
10 minutes

COOKING TIME
45 minutes

2 cups (240 g) roughly chopped mixed almonds, cashews, pecans, walnuts and pumpkin seeds (preferably activated)

2 cups (200 g) rolled oats

2 cups (120 g) coconut flakes

7 tablespoons chia seeds

½ cup (100 g) coconut oil (or butter, or a mixture of both)

¾ cup (175 ml) rice malt syrup

1 cup (250 ml) Pumpkin Puree (see page 23)

1 teaspoon ground cinnamon

1 teaspoon ground allspice

1 teaspoon ground ginger

½ teaspoon ground cloves (optional)

1. Preheat the oven to 160°C (gas 3). Line a rectangular baking tray with baking paper. Combine the nuts, oats, coconut flakes and chia seeds in a large bowl.

2. Stir the coconut oil, rice malt syrup, Pumpkin Puree and spices together in a saucepan over medium heat and bring to a gentle boil. Remove from heat and stir into the nut mixture until well combined.

3. Press the mixture evenly into the prepared baking tray and bake for 30–40 minutes, or until golden and firm to touch in the centre.

4. Remove from the oven and allow to cool before slicing into bars. Store in an airtight container in a cool dry place for 1–2 weeks.

TRICKY TIP

For extra protein feel free to add a couple of tablespoons of protein powder to the dry mix. For a gluten-free option replace oats with puffed quinoa or puffed rice.

STICKY CHICKEN WINGS

Recipe by Di Heath

SERVES 4

PREPARATION TIME

5 minutes

COOKING TIME

35 minutes
(+ 40 minutes
resting)

1 tablespoon rice malt syrup

2 tablespoons soy sauce or tamari

1 heaped teaspoon crushed garlic

10 chicken wings

sour cream or other dipping sauce
(we prefer ours with tzatziki), to serve

1. Preheat the oven to 180°C (gas 4).

2. Place the rice malt syrup, soy sauce or tamari and garlic in a glass jug
    and heat in the microwave for about 10 seconds to melt rice malt syrup,
    then stir to combine.

3. Place the chicken wings into a baking dish and pour the sauce over.
    Turn the wings to coat in the sauce.

4. Bake for 25 minutes, turning a few times during cooking to coat with the
    sauce. Turn the oven off and leave the chicken wings to sit in the warm
    oven for 40 minutes.

5. After 40 minutes turn the oven back on to 220°C (gas 7) and bake
    for 5–10 minutes or until well browned and heated through thoroughly.
    Serve with sour cream or your choice of dipping sauce.

TRICKY TIP

You can leave out the last two steps and just cook them for 40 minutes
if you prefer. However if you do have the extra time you will be rewarded
with the tastiest, fall-off-the-bone, succulent chicken wings ever!

JACKET SWEET POTATO
WITH BUTTERNUT BAKED BEANS

SERVES 4

PREPARATION TIME
5 minutes

COOKING TIME
50 minutes

4 small sweet potatoes
or 2 large ones, halved

2 tablespoons coconut oil

2–3 cups (500–750 ml) Butternut
Baked Beans, heated (see page 58)

½ cup (60 g) grated cheddar cheese

salad leaves, to serve

freshly ground black pepper,
to taste (optional)

1. Preheat the oven to 200°C (gas 6).

2. Rub the sweet potatoes with the coconut oil. Place the sweet potatoes
   on an oven tray and cook for 40–50 minutes until tender.

3. Top the sweet potatoes with warm beans and sprinkle with grated cheese.
   Serve with salad leaves and a grinding of pepper, if you like.

TRICKY TIP

Make this meal for the whole family by multiplying the ingredients
to feed more people.

VEGETARIAN 'SAUSAGE' ROLLS

Recipe by Corinna Rhodes

*These vegetarian 'sausage' rolls are easy to prepare in advance.
Make up a batch and freeze in portions. Remove a few at a time
when a quick and yummy meal is needed.*

MAKES 12

PREPARATION TIME
15 minutes

COOKING TIME
20 minutes

1 onion, roughly chopped

1 cup (115 g) walnuts

1 cup (100 g) rolled oats

4 tablespoons chopped fresh herbs
(oregano, basil, thyme, parsley, dill,
marjoram)

3 eggs

150 g feta

1 tablespoon tamari

½ cup (25 g) breadcrumbs

3 sheets puff pastry

¼ cup (15 g) baby spinach

20 g butter, melted

1. Preheat the oven to 200°C (gas 6). Line a baking tray with baking paper.

2. Place the onion, walnuts, oats and herbs in a food processor and process
    until finely chopped. Add the egg, cheese, tamari and breadcrumbs to the
    mixture and pulse until combined.

3. Lay the pastry on the clean kitchen bench in front of you. Place a layer of
    spinach leaves along one long edge of each pastry half. Place the filling
    mixture on top of the spinach leaves. Roll into log shapes and cut each into
    four equal portions.

4. Place the rolls on the prepared tray and brush with melted butter. Bake for
    20 minutes until crisp and golden.

TRICKY TIP

Keep a few batches of these in the freezer. They are easy to grab for the
lunchbox, snacks or picnics.

RAINY DAY KITCHEN FUN

Use your Rainy Day Kitchen Fun to teach your kids good culinary habits and allow them to bask in the glory of their creations!

FLUFFY RASPBERRY MUFFINS

MAKES 12

PREPARATION TIME
10 minutes

COOKING TIME
30 minutes

2 cups (250 g) gluten-free flour, sifted

2½ teaspoons baking powder

½ teaspoon salt

1 cup (250 ml) unsweetened almond milk (use regular milk or coconut milk to make recipe nut free)

125 g butter, melted

2 eggs, whisked

⅓ cup (75 ml) rice malt syrup

1½ cups (180 g) frozen or fresh raspberries

1. Preheat the oven to 180°C (gas 4). Line a muffin or cupcake tray with 12 paper cases.

2. Combine the sifted flour, baking powder and salt in a large bowl. Pour in the milk, butter, eggs and rice malt syrup. Mix until a batter forms. Gently stir through the raspberries.

3. Spoon the mixture into the prepared paper cases, and bake for 25–30 minutes or until the muffins are well risen and a skewer comes out clean when inserted into the centre.

4. Remove from the tray and allow to cool on a wire rack before serving.

GREEN SLIME LOLLIES

MAKES 8

PREPARATION TIME
5 minutes
(+ 4 hours freezing)

1 cup (50 g) baby spinach leaves

1 cup (125 g) frozen strawberries or blueberries

1 frozen banana, roughly chopped before freezing

4 tablespoons almonds, soaked overnight (or use almond meal)

1½ cups (375 ml) milk (any kind)

1. Blend all the ingredients in a blender and divide between eight ice lolly moulds. Freeze for 4 hours or until firm.

2. To make a green slime smoothie, pour the mixture into two cups or jars. Serve with a straw for fun.

FLUFFY RASPBERRY MUFFINS

DINO COOKIE BITES

DINO COOKIE BITES

MAKES 16

PREPARATION TIME
10 minutes

4 tablespoons natural, sugar-free and salt-free peanut butter

1 tablespoon rice malt syrup

½ cup (125 ml) coconut cream

4 tablespoons coconut oil, melted

½ cup (60 g) coconut flour

⅓ cup (60 g) chilled cooked quinoa

½ teaspoon sea salt flakes

1. Combine the peanut butter, rice malt syrup, coconut cream and coconut oil in a large bowl and mix well.

2. Add the coconut flour, quinoa and salt and mix to form dough. Add a little more coconut flour if the mixture is too soft to form into balls.

3. Pinch off walnut-sized pieces of the dough and roll into balls. Store in an airtight container in the fridge for up to 3 days.

CHOCOLATE CRACKLES

These take us back to when we were in primary school and a classmate would bring in a batch made from the recipe on the back of a cereal box. Enjoy the copha-like (and trans fat-free) flavour from the coconut oil and the crunchy, chocolate puffed cereal. This recipe contains 1 teaspoon of added sugar per serve so we recommend it for a celebration treat.

MAKES 24

PREPARATION TIME
10 minutes
(+ 1 hour setting)

COOKING TIME
5 minutes

4 cups (50 g) low-sugar puffed rice cereal or popped corn kernels (made from popping about 4 tablespoons corn kernels) or 4 cups (120 g) puffed brown rice

4 tablespoons desiccated coconut

1 cup (200 g) coconut oil

4 tablespoons raw cacao powder

1 teaspoon vanilla powder

½ cup (125 ml) rice malt syrup

1. Line two muffin or cupcake trays with 24 paper cases.

2. Combine the puffed cereal and desiccated coconut in a large bowl. Mix well.

3. Heat the coconut oil, cacao, vanilla powder and rice malt syrup in a small saucepan over a low heat and combine thoroughly until melted. Allow to cool slightly, and then pour over the dry ingredients.

4. Stir well, and then spoon into the paper cases. Refrigerate for around an hour or until set. Store in an airtight container in the fridge for up to 1 week.

CHOCOLATE LAVA BROWNIES

Recipe by Milena Zanetti

This recipe contains 1 teaspoon of added sugar per serve so we recommend it for a celebration treat.

MAKES 8

PREPARATION TIME
10 minutes

COOKING TIME
30 minutes

coconut oil, butter or ghee, for greasing

1½ cups (150 g) hazelnut meal

4 tablespoons raw cacao powder

1 teaspoon baking powder

2 eggs

2 tablespoons rice malt syrup

4 tablespoons macadamia oil or coconut oil

4 tablespoons coconut milk

1 teaspoon vanilla extract

2 strawberries, thinly sliced

½ cup (125 ml) Sugar-Free Nut-Ella (see page 23)

1. Preheat the oven to 180°C (gas 4). Grease eight holes of a muffin or cupcake tray.

2. Combine the hazelnut meal, cacao powder and baking powder in a large bowl. Add the eggs, rice malt syrup, oil, milk and vanilla then mix well to form a smooth batter.

3. Spoon into the prepared tray and bake for 25 minutes until the batter has risen and cooked through.

4. Remove from the oven and using a piping bag squeeze the Sugar-Free Nut-Ella into the centre of the brownies until it starts oozing over the top of the brownie. Return to the oven and cook for a further 5 minutes.

5. Remove from the oven and cool in the tray. Serve with a slice of strawberry on top.

> **TRICKY TIP**
>
> Store leftover Sugar-Free Nut-Ella (see page 23) in the fridge, and use as a dipping sauce for strawberries, or pour over a fruit skewer.

COCONUT AND RASPBERRY LOAF

Recipe by Sophie Peters

This is a lovely loaf made by our IQS ambassador Sophie. Serve in lunchboxes or for afternoon tea during the week. Experiment with a pinch of vanilla powder or cinnamon for additional flavour.

MAKES 10

PREPARATION TIME
5 minutes

COOKING TIME
50 minutes

1 cup (120 g) wholemeal self-raising flour

1 cup (250 ml) milk (any kind)

1–3 teaspoons stevia or rice malt syrup or a combination of both

1 cup (120 g) chopped nuts and seeds (try almonds, cashews, sunflower seeds and pumpkin seeds)

½ pear or green apple, grated

¾ cup (75 g) shredded coconut

¼ cup (30 g) frozen raspberries

butter, to serve (optional)

1. Preheat the oven to 180°C (gas 4). Line a 13 cm x 23 cm loaf tin with baking paper.

2. Combine all the ingredients, except the raspberries and butter, in a bowl. Mix well. Add the raspberries and gently fold into the mixture.

3. Pour batter into prepared pan and bake for 40–50 minutes until golden on top. It might seem a bit gooey if you cut into it straight out of the oven but once cooled, it will become firm. Slice and serve on its own or with a smear of butter.

HOT CROSS BUNS

MAKES 8

PREPARATION TIME
1 hour 20 minutes

COOKING TIME
20 minutes

1¼ cups (155 g) gluten-free plain flour or plain flour, plus extra for dusting

¾ cup (90 g) buckwheat flour

⅓ cup (60 g) potato starch

2 teaspoons guar gum or 1½ teaspoons xanthan gum

1 teaspoon salt

3 teaspoons ground cinnamon

1 teaspoon ground nutmeg

1 teaspoon ground cloves

1 tablespoon dry yeast

1 cup (115 g) pecans or walnuts, roughly chopped

2 eggs

4 tablespoons granulated stevia

¾ cup (175 ml) milk or coconut milk

2 tablespoons olive oil, plus extra for greasing

zest of 1 orange, finely grated

zest of 1 lemon, finely grated

EGG GLAZE

1 egg, lightly beaten

WHITE CROSS

2 tablespoons gluten-free plain flour or plain flour

2 tablespoons water

1. Sift the flours, potato starch, gum, salt and spices into a large bowl. Mix in the yeast and nuts.

2. In a second bowl, beat the eggs with the stevia, milk, oil and zests.

3. Add the egg mixture to the dry ingredients and mix well until dough forms. Transfer the dough to a clean, lightly greased bowl and set aside, covered, in a warm place for one hour to let the dough rise.

4. Preheat the oven to 180°C (gas 4). Line a baking tray with baking paper. Turn the risen dough out onto a lightly floured surface and knead for one minute.

5. Divide dough into eight, roll into even balls. Place them on the prepared tray, allow to sit for 15 minutes and then brush with the egg glaze.

6. Make the white cross mixture by combining the flour and water to form a thick paste. Place the mixture in a small ziplock bag and snip off a tiny bit of one corner. Pipe the paste onto the buns to make crosses.

7. Bake for 20 minutes or until golden. Serve warm or cool on a wire rack. These buns are best enjoyed on the day they are made.

GLUTEN-FREE CHOC-CHIP COOKIES

These cookies are deliciously tasty and almost cake-like in texture. Enjoy warm out of the oven, or cold if you prefer.

MAKES 12

PREPARATION TIME
10 minutes

COOKING TIME
20 minutes

1½ cups (180 g) buckwheat flour

1 teaspoon baking powder

1 teaspoon vanilla powder

½ teaspoon sea salt

125 g unsalted butter, softened

½ cup (125 ml) rice malt syrup

1 egg

100 g 85% dark chocolate, coarsely chopped (you can add a pinch of stevia to counteract the dark chocolate for younger kids) or good-quality dark chocolate chips

1. Preheat the oven to 160°C (gas 3). Line two baking trays with baking paper.

2. Combine the flour, baking powder, vanilla powder and salt in a large bowl.

3. In a separate bowl beat the butter and rice malt syrup with an electric mixer until creamy. Add egg and beat until combined.

4. Add the butter mixture to the dry ingredients and combine with a wooden spoon. Fold through the chocolate (and stevia if using).

5. Roll tablespoons of the mixture into balls and place 4 cm apart on the lined trays. Press down slightly.

6. Bake for 15–20 minutes until lightly golden. Transfer to a wire rack to cool. Store in an airtight container for up to 3 days.

PRINCESS CUPCAKES

Recipe by Georgia Harding

These cupcakes are actually best eaten the next day, especially if you think you can taste the beans or egg. They can also be frozen in an airtight container or ziplock bag. This recipe contains 1 teaspoon of added sugar per serve so we recommend it for a celebration treat.

MAKES 6

PREPARATION TIME
15 minutes

COOKING TIME
10 minutes

1 × 425 g can cannellini beans, drained and well rinsed

5 large eggs

1 tablespoon vanilla powder

50 g butter, softened

4 tablespoons rice malt syrup

40 g coconut flour (weigh this, as it really needs to be exact)

1 teaspoon baking powder

½ teaspoon bicarbonate of soda

¼ teaspoon sea salt

VANILLA ICING

50 g butter, softened

1 tablespoon rice malt syrup

1 tablespoon vanilla powder

pinch of granulated stevia

1. Preheat the oven to 180°C (gas 4). Line a cupcake or muffin tray with paper cases or baking paper.

2. In a powerful blender or food processor, puree the rinsed beans, eggs and vanilla until very smooth and set aside. *Note: Don't scrimp on the eggs or let the batter sit for too long. Not enough eggs and delaying getting it in the oven will result in a much heavier batter and cake.*

3. Next mix together the butter and rice malt syrup with a wooden spoon until very well combined. Add to the pureed mix and combine well. Now add the coconut flour, baking powder, bicarbonate of soda and salt.

4. Spoon the mixture into the prepared tray immediately. The batter does have a slightly thick but airy consistency, which is unusual if you've never worked with coconut flour before.

5. Bake for 20 minutes or until lightly brown on top and springy to touch. Set aside to cool on a wire rack.

6. To make the vanilla icing beat all the ingredients together until light and fluffy. Once cupcakes are completely cool, ice and serve.

LUNCHBOX IDEAS

Making your kids' lunchbox exciting
is half the challenge! Here, a few clever
ideas along with some tips for navigating
the school tuckshop.

WHAT'S THE BEST LUNCHBOX?

- **Use brown paper bags or paper:** They're a simple way to avoid plastic and encourage recycling. Avoid the greaseproof variety.

- **Clingfilm:** The good news is plastics have dramatically improved now they are not made from PVC, so use them if need be.

- **Check the numbers on plastic containers:** Always check the number in the little triangle on the bottom – 2, 4 and 5 are safe. Avoid the rest.

- **Glass and ceramic containers:** These are ideal and really practical; however be wary of giving them to young children who are likely to throw their school bags around like a football.

- **Ziplock bags are easy to reuse.** Simply rinse with hot soapy water and hang to dry on the washing line or near the sink.

- **Refillable drink bottles:** Ditch the plastics altogether. Refillable stainless steel drink bottles encourage kids to enjoy tap water right throughout the day. Being BPA free, they're a safe substitute for the disposable plastic varieties.

GET ECO-FRIENDLY

Consider ditching paper and plastic bags altogether and pack kids' lunches in reusable, eco-friendly containers such as food-grade stainless steel lunch containers that can be used throughout the school year.

Minimise waste.
Try to eliminate quick fix pre-packaged lunches so that only compostable scraps like apple cores and banana peels remain after eating.

Our guide to a healthy lunchbox

We get asked this all the time . . . what to pack for kids' lunches. We checked it out for you, and here's what each lunchbox should (ultimately) contain:

- **A portion of grains or slow-release carbohydrates:** one slice of sourdough bread the size of a CD cover or half a tennis ball worth of cooked quinoa.

- **A portion of protein:** a piece of chicken or beef the approximate size of a deck of cards.

- **A portion of dairy:** 1 cup (250 ml) of milk or a small tub of unsweetened yoghurt.
- **Two portions of vegetables:** a handful of cooked veggies or salad.
- **A portion of fruit:** low-fructose fruit like kiwi fruit.

A sample lunchbox idea:

- Start with a frozen green smoothie (veggies); use it as an ice brick to keep food cool. It'll be nice and slushy-like for a mid-morning treat.
- Include a small tub of unsweetened full-fat yoghurt (dairy) and encourage your kids to stir through a handful of berries (fruit).
- For lunch, load up a wholegrain sandwich (carbs) with salad greens (more veggies) and shredded roast chicken (protein) with skin (fat).
- Top it off with a litre of water.

Cookie cutters make everyday food irresistible.
Use crazy shapes to transform a sandwich, cheese slices or cucumber chunks into your kids' favourite thing!

Swaps

If you're stuck for ideas, why not try some of these simple swaps for a kick start.

SWAP THIS	FOR THIS
Sandwich	Cheesy Green Fritters (see page 44)
Store-bought breakfast drink	Up and At 'Em Breakfast Whip (see page 36) Note: omit nut butter for lunchboxes.
Potato crisps	Salt and Vinegar Kale Crisps (see page 52) or Roasted Root Vegetable Crisps (see page 104)
Café-style banana bread	Coconut and Raspberry Loaf (see page 73) Note: omit nuts for lunchboxes.
Apple puree	Fluffy Carrot Mousse (see page 43)
Roll-ups	Ants on a Log (see page 108) Note: substitute nut butter with cream cheese.

What about the tuckshop?!

Your kids will be pleased to know we're not suggesting a full ban. There are ways to steer your kids' choices in a healthier direction while still letting them have the thrill of ordering from the tuckshop.

We've given you a canteen list (from a real school) below, and ticked the foods that would be IQS approved. 'Hooray!' we hear you say.

BREAKFAST
Toast – ½ Muffin
(vegemite, cheese, honey, jam)
Hot Chocolate
Asst Drinks

SANDWICHES & SALADS
✓ Vegemite
Baked Beans
Spaghetti
✓ Cheese
Creamed Corn
✓ Egg *(Plain/Curried)*
✓ Salad
✓ Tuna
✓ Red Salmon
✓ Ham
✓ BBQ Chicken
✓ Ham & Salad
✓ BBQ Chicken & Salad
✓ Tuna & Salad
✓ Salmon & Salad
✓ Salad Container
Extra Filling

HOT FOOD
✓ Chicken Wrap
(chicken/lettuce/tomato/cheese)
Hamburger
(low-fat burger/lettuce/tomato)
✓ Chicken Burger
(chicken/lettuce/mayonnaise)
✓ Lasagne – beef or vegetable
✓ Pie
Sausage Roll
✓ Cheese & Bacon Bread
Pizza *(ham/pineapple)*
Pizza *(cheese/bacon)*
✓ Corn on Cob
Yummy Drummy
Party Pie
Tomato sauce

SNACKS
Honey/Soy Chips
Corntos
Burgermen
Chicken Crackers
Fini Roller
Noodles
Spiral Apple
Snakes
Licorice
Faces
Yoghurt Babies
Bears

DRINKS
Milkshakes
Focus Water
(raspberry, blackcurrant, lemonade, fruity fix)
✓ Bottled Water
Big M Milk
(chocolate, strawberry)
Orange & Mango Popper
Apple & Blackcurrant Popper
Apple/Orange Juice Cup
Apple & Blackcurrant

ICE CREAMS
Milo Shake
Lifesaver
Slushies
Moosies
Billabong
Icy Pole
Icey Bite
Yogo Ice
Jelly Stick
TNT Sour

Generally, things to steer clear of include:

- soft drinks
- flavoured milk
- dried fruit
- fruit buns
- white bread
- sultanas
- foods lathered in sauces

ROAST BEEF WRAP WITH GREEN RICOTTA SMASH

SERVES 1

PREPARATION TIME
5 minutes

4 tablespoons cooked peas

½ cup (120 g) ricotta

1 tablespoon mint leaves, chopped (optional)

sea salt, to taste

1 gluten-free wrap

50 g roast beef, from the deli (or you can use leftovers)

½ cup (25 g) baby spinach leaves

1. Combine the peas, ricotta and mint in a small bowl and mash using a fork until smooth. Season with salt.

2. Spread the centre of the wrap with the green smash. Top with the roast beef and baby spinach. Roll up to serve.

PARMA HAM ROLL UPS

Recipe by Lee Holmes

MAKES 8

PREPARATION TIME
5 minutes

1 green apple

4 tablespoons soft goat's cheese

4 slices parma ham, sliced in half

1. Slice the apple into thin slices, about 5 mm thick. Spread a thin layer of goat's cheese on each slice.

2. Lay a slice of parma ham on a flat surface, and place the apple with cheese on one end.

3. Roll from the edge of the parma ham with the apple and continue rolling so the apple is encased. Repeat with the remaining apple and parma ham.

DUNKABLE CHOCOLATE CREAMS

MAKES 16

PREPARATION TIME
15 minutes

COOKING TIME
10 minutes

1 cup (125 g) gluten-free self-raising flour, plus extra for dusting

⅓ cup (40 g) raw cacao powder

2 tablespoons granulated stevia

75 g cold butter, diced

4 tablespoons milk

1 tablespoon rice malt syrup

FILLING

125 g cream cheese, softened

25 g butter, softened

1 tablespoon rice malt syrup

½ teaspoon vanilla powder

1. Preheat the oven to 180°C (gas 4). Line a baking tray with baking paper.

2. Combine the flour, cacao and stevia in a large bowl or food processor. Add the diced cold butter and rub together using your fingers or process until the mixture resembles fine breadcrumbs.

3. Add the milk and rice malt syrup and mix or process to form dough.

4. Transfer the mixture to a lightly floured surface and knead for another minute or so, until the dough is nice and smooth.

5. Flatten the dough and place between two sheets of baking paper. Using a rolling pin, roll the dough out to about 4–5 mm thick.

6. Cut out rounds or flowers using a 3 cm cookie cutter, and transfer to the prepared baking tray. Reroll the dough scraps as necessary.

7. Prick each biscuit with a fork a few times. Bake for 10 minutes or until firm then transfer to a wire rack to cool.

8. To make the filling, whisk the cream cheese until light and creamy, then add the butter, rice malt syrup and vanilla powder and whisk until combined.

9. To assemble the biscuit, place about 2 teaspoons of filling on the middle of half of the biscuits. Top with the remaining biscuits and squeeze together to push the filling to the edges.

YAY LUNCH!

YUM!

EGGY SCROLLS

SERVES 1

PREPARATION TIME
5 minutes

2 eggs

2 tablespoons milk

1½ teaspoons chia seeds

1 teaspoon olive oil

1 organic wrap

2–3 tablespoons mayonnaise or Pumpkin Puree (see page 23)

1. Beat the egg for 1 minute, then stir in the milk and chia seeds.

2. Heat the oil in a frying pan big enough to make quite a thin omelette over medium heat. Pour the egg mixture into the pan and cook for 2–3 minutes until set.

3. Spread the wrap with the mayonnaise or Pumpkin Puree.

4. Put the omelette on top and roll up into a log to serve.

BERRY DELICIOUS CHIA PUDDING

MAKES 2

PREPARATION TIME
5 minutes
(+ overnight)

½ cup (75 g) chia seeds

1½ cups (375 ml) milk (any kind)

½ teaspoon vanilla powder
or 2 teaspoons vanilla extract

pinch of granulated stevia,
to taste

4 tablespoons berries, fresh or frozen

1. Combine all the ingredients except the berries in a bowl. Divide between two jars. Place puddings in the fridge overnight.

2. In the morning, top with the berries and store in a cooler bag or lunchbox for school lunches.

CHEESY COURGETTE CUPCAKES

MAKES 12

PREPARATION TIME
15 minutes

COOKING TIME
45 minutes

coconut oil, butter or ghee, for greasing

2 large courgettes

1 teaspoon sea salt

500 g ricotta cheese

1 cup (100 g) shaved or grated parmesan

2 spring onions, finely chopped

2 garlic cloves, crushed

4 tablespoons chopped dill

zest of 1 lemon

3 large eggs, well beaten

100 g crumbled feta

1. Preheat the oven to 170°C (gas 3). Grease a 12-hole muffin tray with the oil and line with paper cases.

2. Grate the courgettes using a food processor with a shredding disc or hand-held grater to give you 2 cups (500 ml) grated courgettes. Combine the courgettes and salt in a colander or sturdy sieve and let sit for 15 minutes. Use your fingers or a spoon to press out as much moisture as possible.

3. Combine the ricotta, parmesan, spring onions, garlic, dill and lemon zest, then stir in the eggs and courgettes.

4. Pour the mixture into the prepared muffin tray and top with the feta. Bake for 35 minutes. Remove from the tray and allow the cupcakes to cool completely on a wire rack so they set properly.

> **TRICKY TIP**
>
> Freeze these cupcakes in portions of two in ziplock bags. Place in lunchboxes straight from the freezer. They'll have thawed by the time lunchbreak comes around.

YOGHURT DOUGH SCROLLS

Recipe by Kasia Froncek

This is a great substitute for those sugar-laden cream buns from the local bakery. Play with different variations and your kids will never ask for the store-bought version again!

MAKES 6–8

PREPARATION TIME
15 minutes

COOKING TIME
25 minutes

DOUGH

1⅓ cups (165 g) self-raising flour, plus extra for dusting

1 cup (250 ml) Greek yoghurt

Additional topping ingredients (see below)

1. Preheat the oven to 180°C (gas 4). Line a baking tray with baking paper.

2. For the dough, mix the flour and the yoghurt in a bowl until they start to come together into a ball.

3. Turn the dough out onto a well-floured surface and knead for about 5 minutes. Divide into six or eight equal portions. Flatten out a little with your hands; add more flour as needed to keep dough from sticking. Take a portion and roll into a long thin rectangle – about a centimetre thick.

4. Top dough with your chosen filling and roll dough into a scroll. Place on baking tray.

5. Repeat process until all the dough is gone. Sprinkle additional ingredients on top of scrolls and bake for 25 minutes or until golden and cooked through.

VARIATIONS

Cinnamon and walnut scrolls

Note: These can't be taken to school as they contain nuts.

- To the dough mixture add 2 teaspoons rice malt syrup and 1 teaspoon cinnamon.
- Once the dough is rolled, spread the dough with unsalted butter, sprinkle with chopped walnuts and cinnamon, then drizzle with a little rice malt syrup.

Pizza scrolls

Spread the dough with Homemade Tomato Sauce (see page 18) or low-sugar tomato puree, top with chopped ham or bacon, sliced cherry tomatoes, diced peppers and grated cheese.

BUCKET CHICKEN WITH MUSHY PEA MASH

For a cheesy variation on this recipe, serve up the Bucket Chicken with Cauli-cream Cheese Sauce (see page 26).

SERVES 8

PREPARATION TIME
5 minutes

COOKING TIME
40 minutes

Mushy Pea Mash (see page 26)

8 chicken drumsticks

1 cup (125 g) plain flour

2 eggs, whisked

2 cups (250 g) panko breadcrumbs

40–60 g butter, melted

1 tablespoon sesame seeds

salad, to serve

1. Preheat the oven to 200°C (gas 6). Line a baking tray with baking paper.

2. Make Mushy Pea Mash. Set aside to cool.

3. Place the flour, eggs and breadcrumbs in three separate bowls.

4. Coat the chicken in flour, then egg, then breadcrumbs. Place onto the prepared tray and drizzle over the butter. Sprinkle with sesame seeds and bake for 40 minutes, turning the drumsticks after 20 minutes.

5. To serve, wrap 1–2 drumsticks in foil and pack into a lunchbox with an ice cooler or frozen smoothie. Include salad and a container of Mushy Pea Mash.

PUMPKIN MUFFINS

MAKES 8

PREPARATION TIME
10 minutes

COOKING TIME
20 minutes

2 cups (250 g) gluten-free self-raising flour

1 teaspoon bicarbonate of soda

sea salt and freshly ground black pepper, to taste

1 cup (115 g) grated cheddar cheese

1 courgette, grated, extra moisture squeezed out

½ cup (20 g) finely chopped basil

4 tablespoons finely sliced chives

2 eggs

1 cup (250 ml) Pumpkin Puree (see page 23)

1. Preheat the oven to 200°C (gas 6). Line eight holes of a muffin pan with baking paper or paper cases.

2. Sift the flour, bicarbonate of soda, salt and pepper into a large bowl. Add the cheese, courgette and herbs.

3. Whisk the egg and pumpkin in a jug until well combined.

4. Make a well in the centre of the dry ingredients. Pour in the egg mixture. Using a large metal spoon, gently mix until just combined. Spoon into muffin holes.

5. Bake for 15–20 minutes or until a skewer inserted into the centre comes out clean. Stand in pan for 3 minutes. Turn onto a wire rack to cool. Store in an airtight container at room temperature.

GNOME IN A CAVE

Recipe by Ruby Gallery at paleoforkids.com.au

MAKES 8

PREPARATION TIME
10 minutes

COOKING TIME
35 minutes

coconut oil, butter or ghee, for greasing

1 teaspoon coconut oil

1 onion, finely chopped

1 green apple, peeled, cored and finely chopped

2 bay leaves

2 teaspoons ground cumin

1 teaspoon ground coriander

1 teaspoon ground cinnamon

1 teaspoon ground ginger or ½ teaspoon grated fresh ginger

500 g beef mince

1 carrot, grated

4 tablespoons breadcrumbs

3 eggs

200 ml coconut milk

1 teaspoon ground turmeric

sea salt and freshly ground black pepper, to taste

1. Preheat the oven to 160°C (gas 3). Grease eight ramekins or eight holes of a muffin tray.

2. Heat the coconut oil in a frying pan over medium heat and cook the onion until tender.

3. Add the apple, bay leaves, cumin, coriander, cinnamon and ginger and cook for 3 minutes. Transfer the onion and apple mixture from the pan to a bowl. Discard the bay leaves. Add the mince to the pan and fry until cooked through adding salt and pepper to taste.

4. Add the mince to the apple and onion mixture, along with the grated carrot and breadcrumbs. Mix well.

5. In a separate bowl, beat the eggs together with the coconut milk, turmeric and a bit of salt until frothy.

6. Divide the meat mixture evenly between the ramekins or muffin tray holes. They should be about two-thirds full. Pour the egg mixture over the top.

7. Cook for 20–30 minutes, until the top is golden and the egg mixture is cooked through. Rest the muffins for 10 minutes before turning out of the tray.

TRICKY TIP

You can substitute the coconut milk with almond milk. Sneak in more vegetables by finely chopping pumpkin and/or courgettes and adding in step two. If your kids are egg intolerant you can omit the egg topping and simply top the ramekins with mashed cooked sweet potatoes.

GRAB 'N' RUN

We've put together a bunch of recipes for active kids on the go — easy to grab off a picnic rug and eat while playing in the backyard.

CUCUMBER LAUGHING HEADS

MAKES 6

PREPARATION TIME
5 minutes

1 cucumber or 2 ridge cucumbers

4 tablespoons cream cheese, softened

50 g thinly sliced ham

1 teaspoon capers

1. Cut the cucumber in half lengthways and scoop out the seeds with a teaspoon.

2. Fill one 'tunnel' with cream cheese and the other with a thin layer of ham. Press the two layers together then slice carefully into 3 cm rounds.

3. Place two capers on the cream cheese for eyes.

TRICKY TIP

Add some fronds of fennel to make eyebrows.

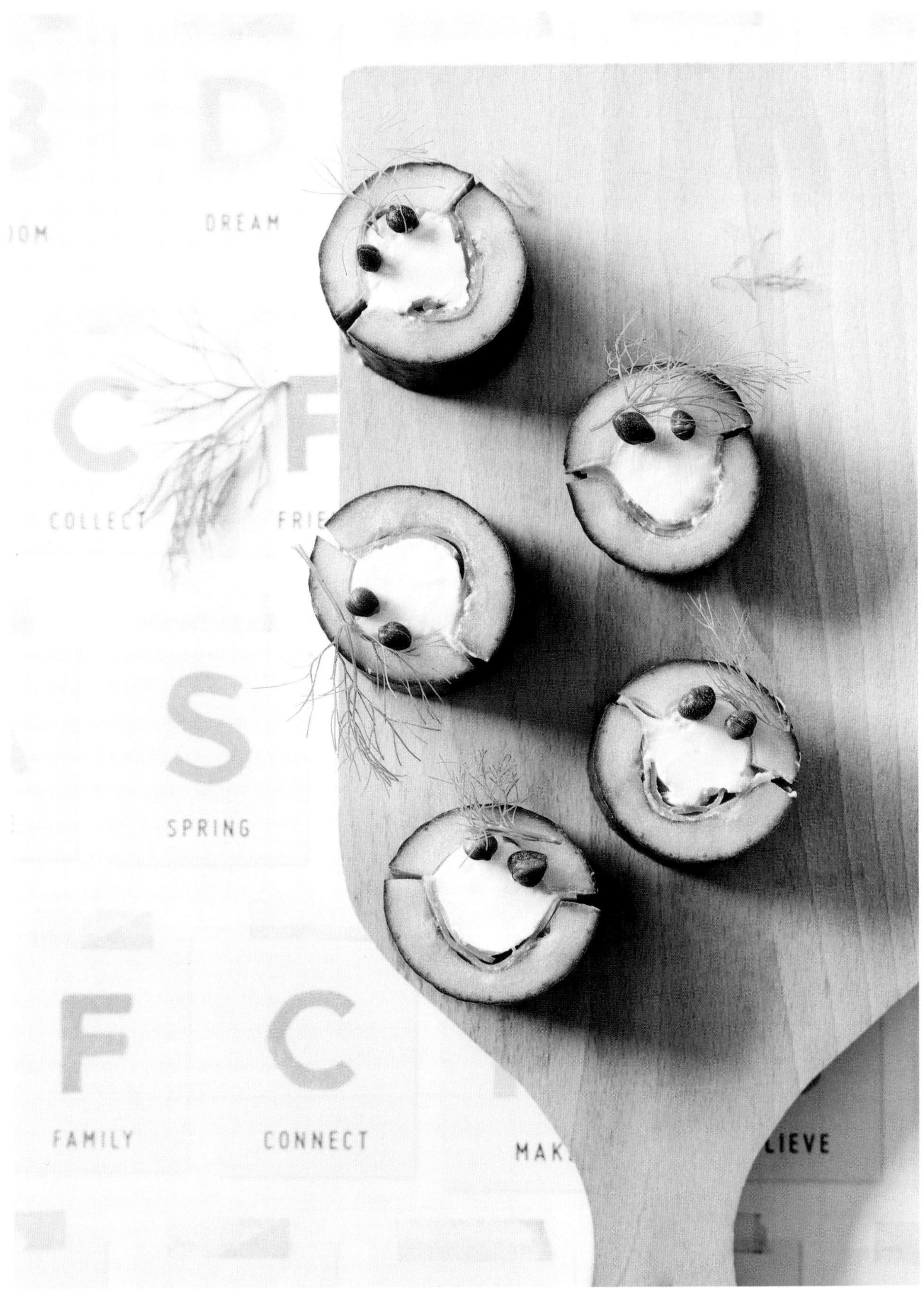
DREAM
COLLECT
SPRING
FAMILY
CONNECT

NUTTY TEETH

SERVES 2

as a snack

PREPARATION TIME

5 minutes

**1 red or green apple,
cut into thin wedges**

**1–2 tablespoons nut butter
(peanut, almond, cashew)**

**2 teaspoons flaked almonds
or pumpkin seeds**

1. Spread the nut butter over half of the apple slices and stick on another slice at a 'jaw-like' angle.

2. Spike the almond flakes or pumpkin seeds into the nut butter to form teeth.

ROASTED ROOT VEGETABLE CRISPS

MAKES A large
bowlful

PREPARATION TIME
10 minutes

COOKING TIME
25 minutes

1 parsnip, peeled

1 swede, peeled

1 beetroot, peeled

1 sweet potato, peeled

2 tablespoons olive oil

sea salt and freshly ground black pepper, to taste

1. Preheat the oven to 200°C (gas 6). Line two trays with baking paper.

2. Slice all the vegetables into even thin 'crisp-like' rounds using a sharp knife or a mandoline.

3. Place the parsnip and swede 'crisps' in a bowl and drizzle with half of the olive oil, toss to coat. Transfer to one of the baking trays spreading the crisps in a single layer.

4. Repeat the process with the beetroot and sweet potato and place on the other tray. Season with salt and pepper.

5. Bake the parsnip and swede crisps for around 15 minutes and the beetroot and sweet potato crisps for 25 minutes, or until golden. Remove from oven and transfer to wire racks to cool.

CHEESE AND BACON LOLLIPOPS

MAKES 8

PREPARATION TIME
10 minutes
(+ chilling)

COOKING TIME
5 minutes

½ cup (120 g) cream cheese, softened

½ cup (60 g) grated cheddar or crumbled goat's cheese

4 tablespoons chopped herbs (thyme or basil are great)

sea salt and freshly ground black pepper, to taste

4 rashers bacon

3–4 tablespoons crushed pecans or almonds

1. Combine the cheeses, half the herbs, salt and pepper in a bowl.

2. Divide into eight bite-sized pieces, roll into balls and insert a bamboo skewer into each ball. Refrigerate overnight or freeze for 20 minutes.

3. Meanwhile, cook the bacon until crispy. Allow to cool then dice finely or crumble up and mix with the crushed nuts and the remaining herbs. Roll the balls in the bacon and nut mixture and serve.

Little hands like little handles.
Lamb chops are sweet, chicken drumsticks are juicy and cocktail sticks add a handle to any fruit, sandwich or meat.

ANTS ON A LOG

This is a fun, quick snack for the kids. The protein-rich nut butter will keep them going until dinner.

SERVES 2

PREPARATION TIME
5 minutes

2 x 20 cm stalks celery

2 tablespoons nut butter of your choice (peanut, almond or cashew)

1 teaspoon black chia seeds

1. Rinse the celery to clean away any grit.

2. Spread nut butter evenly in the hollow part of the celery.

3. Sprinkle the chia seeds on top to look like ants.

> **TRICKY TIP**
>
> To pack for day trips or picnics cut celery stick into three even lengths and place in a BPA-free plastic container.

LET'S PARTY

This is the chapter of party foods but don't take this as a licence to go to town! These recipes include a slightly higher serving of sugar, so we recommend saving these treats for celebrations and special occasions.

GINGERBREAD SMOOTHIE

SERVES 2

PREPARATION TIME
5 minutes

4–5 ice cubes

2 leftover Hazelnut Cookies, crumbled (see page 123)

4 tablespoons rolled oats

1 scoop vanilla protein powder (optional)

1 teaspoon rice malt syrup

1 teaspoon ground cinnamon

1 teaspoon ground ginger or ½ teaspoon finely grated fresh ginger

2–3 drops liquid stevia (optional)

1 cup (250 ml) unsweetened almond milk

1. Place all the ingredients in a blender (keeping some crumbled cookies for later) and blend until smooth and thick.

2. Pour smoothies into two glasses or jars and top with the reserved crumbled hazelnut cookies.

RASPBERRY LEMONADE JELLIES

SERVES 15

PREPARATION TIME
10 minutes
(+ 1 hour setting)

COOKING TIME
10 minutes

4½ tablespoons Gut Lovin' Gelatin powder

1½ cups (185 g) raspberries, fresh or frozen

zest and juice of 1 lemon

1. Dissolve the gelatin in ⅓ cup (75 ml) cold water and let it sit for 5 minutes until it has become gel-like.

2. Heat the raspberries and lemon juice in a saucepan until almost boiling. Remove from the heat and blitz with a hand-held blender until smooth. Then stir in the gelatin until it has dissolved.

3. Pour into a 10 cm x 15 cm glass or plastic container. Refrigerate for 1 hour until set, then cut into squares. Store in the fridge in an airtight container for up to a week.

GINGERBREAD SMOOTHIE

COCONUT BALLS

MAKES 14

PREPARATION TIME
1 hour 30 minutes

COOKING TIME
5 minutes

100 g 85–90% dark chocolate, roughly chopped

FILLING

2½ cups (185 g) unsweetened shredded coconut

2 tablespoons rice malt syrup

2 tablespoons coconut oil, melted

4 tablespoons coconut milk

1. Line a baking tray with baking paper. Place all the filling ingredients in the food processor. Pulse until the mixture comes together but still has texture. Roll tablespoons of the mixture into round balls and freeze for at least an hour until firm.

2. Meanwhile melt the chocolate over a small saucepan of gently simmering water. Do not let the bowl touch the water. Remove the coconut balls from the freezer and roll them in the melted chocolate so they are completely coated.

3. Place balls on a tray lined with baking paper and sit in the fridge to set before serving. Store in the freezer in an airtight container for up to 1 month.

> **TRICKY TIP**
> These balls will require refrigeration.

CHRISTMAS REINDEER POPS AND SNOWMEN

Recipe by Bree Hateley

MAKES 20

PREPARATION TIME
20 minutes

1½ cups (115 g) desiccated coconut, plus extra for rolling

1 cup (135 g) cashews

1 cup (125 g) macadamias

1 cup (100 g) rolled oats

½ teaspoon ground cinnamon

1 teaspoon vanilla powder or ½ teaspoon vanilla essence

4 tablespoons rice malt syrup

juice of ½ orange

8 tablespoons combined total of goji berries, pecans and cacao nibs, processed to a coarse texture

walnut pieces, goji berries, pumpkin seeds and sunflower seeds, to decorate

1. Place coconut, cashews, macadamias, oats, cinnamon and vanilla in a food processor. Pulse until combined. Add the rice malt syrup and orange juice and whizz again. Gently mix in the goji berries, pecans and cacao nibs.

2. Roll the mixture into balls, roll in coconut and place in fridge for 10 minutes or until firm.

3. To make reindeers, place balls on sticks and decorate with walnut 'ears' and goji berry 'noses'. To make snowmen, stick three balls together with toothpicks, add toothpick arms and decorate with goji berries, pumpkin seeds and sunflower seeds.

4. Store the decorated balls in the fridge for another 10 minutes to set.

TRICKY TIP

These pops are best kept in the fridge for a couple of weeks. If you'd like to keep them for longer, freeze them after a day or two.

CARAMEL POPCORN

MAKES 4 cups
(50 g)

PREPARATION TIME
5 minutes

COOKING TIME
10 minutes

4 cups (50 g) air popped popcorn or 4 tablespoons raw kernels

2 tablespoons rice malt syrup

4 tablespoons coconut milk

3 tablespoons nut butter (cashew, almond or peanut)

1. Place the popped popcorn in a large bowl, or pop your own following the directions on the package.

2. Combine the rice malt syrup and coconut milk in a saucepan over low heat until smooth.

3. Stir in the nut butter. Remove from the heat. Pour the caramel mixture over the popcorn and stir in the bowl until coated.

4. Serve warm or place bowl in the freezer to cool and set.

 Mum's THE WORD

Set up a 'Popcorn Bar'.
Make your kids' next birthday party extra special. Set out several flavours of popped corn (think quirky and fun for the children) and serve children their own individual cups in the flavours of their choice.

DIVINE ORANGE CAKE

Recipe by Sha at sugarfreekids.com.au

MAKES 1 large cake

PREPARATION TIME
20 minutes

COOKING TIME
3 ½ hours

**2 whole oranges, preferably organic
as you use the whole lot**

6 eggs

2½ cups (250 g) almond meal

1½ teaspoons baking powder

1 teaspoon granulated stevia

4 tablespoons rice malt syrup

ICING

1 tablespoon coconut oil

5 tablespoons coconut cream

1 tablespoon rice malt syrup

toasted coconut, to serve

pomegranate seeds, to serve

1. Place the oranges in a saucepan and cover with water, bring to the boil then reduce heat to low and cover and simmer for 2 hours. The oranges should now be very soft. Set aside and allow to cool completely. (You can do this step ahead of time.)

2. Preheat the oven to 160°C (gas 3) and grease and line a 23 cm spring form tin. Cut the top and tail off each orange, discard. Chop remainder of orange into pieces, discard any pips and place into a food processor, skin and all. Process on high speed for about 30 seconds until you have a very smooth bright orange puree.

3. Add the egg, almond meal, stevia, baking powder and rice malt syrup to the food processor with the puree and mix on a medium speed for about 20 seconds until the mixture is well combined. Pour the batter into the prepared tin and bake for about 90 minutes until a skewer comes out clean. Cool in the tin.

4. Meanwhile, make the icing by melting the coconut oil for approximately 10 seconds in the microwave and stirring together with the coconut cream and rice malt syrup. Refrigerate icing until it thickens.

5. Ice the cooled cake with a spatula or the back of a tablespoon. Sprinkle with the toasted coconut and pomegranate seeds.

> **VARIATION**
>
> If you prefer a higher-looking cake, cook it in a well-greased and lined small stainless steel mixing bowl instead. Serve upside down like a dome.

ECHIDNA POPS

Recipe by Alice Nicholls at thewholedaily.com.au
These cheeky little Aussie 'pops' are filled with a healthy trail-mix and barely sweetened. The oats and seeds help to regulate your little ones' blood sugar levels while helping them feel full so they don't over-indulge.

MAKES 20

PREPARATION TIME
1 hour 30 minutes

COOKING TIME
10 minutes

TRAIL MIX

1 cup (100 g) rolled oats

1 cup (30 g) puffed amaranth or quinoa, plus extra for dipping

1 tablespoon goji berries

½ cup (60 g) sesame seeds

4 tablespoons pumpkin seeds

2 tablespoons coconut oil, melted

2 tablespoons nut butter

2 tablespoons rice malt syrup

CHOCOLATE COATING

2 tablespoons raw cacao powder

40 g cacao butter, melted

1 tablespoon rice malt syrup

desiccated coconut, for dipping (optional)

1. Place all the dry trail mix ingredients in the food processor and pulse three or four times so the mix is still rough but combined.

2. Mix together the melted coconut oil, nut butter and rice malt syrup in a bowl over a small saucepan of simmering water. Combine hot mixture with the dry ingredients and set aside for 5–10 minutes to cool and become 'sticky'.

3. Use an ice-cube tray and put a little bit of trail mix into the bottom, add half a straw and press more trail mix around the straw as tightly as possible. Set in the fridge for at least one hour.

4. For the chocolate coating, combine the cacao powder, melted cacao butter and rice malt syrup in a bowl over a small saucepan of simmering water, stirring until completely combined. Allow to cool and thicken slightly.

5. Take the 'pops' out of the fridge and remove gently from the ice-cube tray, drizzle with chocolate to coat. Dip into extra puffed amaranth, quinoa or desiccated coconut to finish.

TRICKY TIP

Wrap an old tissue box with paper and poke holes in the top to make your tray for the pops to stand in. Use straws cut in half for the handles.

GINGERADE

This is a fermented drink . . . which means it doesn't just taste great, it also bubbles like a fizzy drink and is so tremendously good for everyone's guts. You can learn about the health benefits of ferments on my website SarahWilson.com.

It also means it contains table sugar. Table sugar? Yes! It's almost always used for making fermented sodas, but the fructose is 'eaten up' in the process by yeast and bacteria, to create lactic acid and carbonation. Lactic acid is a probiotic that helps digestion, supports the immune system and hydrates cells.

I was a little dubious about whether all of the sugar was used up in this process and did a lot of research into the matter. It seems that, after a 48-hour fermentation period, 80 per cent of the sugar has been gobbled up by the yeast and bacteria. Extrapolated, this means 25 g sugar is left in 2 litres of gingerade. In 1 cup (250 ml) of the stuff, it's 3.1 g sugar, which is about ¾ teaspoon. If consumed with soda water (we find it works best half gingerade, half soda), then one large glass will contain less than ½ teaspoon sugar.

MAKES 2 litres

PREPARATION TIME
10 minutes
(4–5 days
fermenting)

COOKING TIME
10 minutes

6 cups (1.5 litres) water

½ cup (100 g) sugar and ¼ cup (60 ml) rice malt syrup OR ¾ cup (175 ml) rice malt syrup and no sugar

1 cup (100 g) thinly sliced unpeeled fresh ginger

zest and juice of 2 lemons

½ cup (125 ml) whey (the excess liquid from yoghurt)

1. Pour the water into a saucepan, then mix the sugar, syrup and ginger together and stir into the water. Bring to the boil and simmer for 10 minutes.

2. Cool to body temperature then add the lemon zest and juice. (If you have a blender, trim the zest off the lemons and blitz, then trim away the pith and discard, along with any visible pips, then add the lemon flesh to the blender and blitz again.) Transfer to a Mason jar and add the whey.

3. Stir well and allow to sit on the worktop, stirring occasionally, for 2–3 days in hot weather, or until slightly bubbly and becoming tart. Strain the gingerade into glass bottles.

4. Allow to carbonate for another 2–3 days at room temperature, chill, then consume. If you're not going to drink it straight away, keep it in the fridge – it will keep fermenting, even in the cold, and last a week in the fridge before it goes vinegary. The longer it's left to ferment, the tangier it will get.

CHOCOLATE HAZELNUT ICE CREAM SANDWICHES

The ice cream is best made overnight or with at least 4–6 hours freezing time to spare.

MAKES 8–10

PREPARATION TIME
25 minutes
(+ overnight freezing)

COOKING TIME
20 minutes

CHOCOLATE ICE CREAM

1 cup (135 g) hazelnuts

1 cup (250 ml) coconut milk

4 tablespoons rice malt syrup

2 tablespoons raw cacao powder

HAZELNUT COOKIES

½ cup (70 g) hazelnuts (prepared the night before)

3 tablespoons olive oil

1 tablespoon granulated stevia

1 tablespoon vanilla powder

1 cup (100 g) almond meal

pinch of salt

1 egg, whisked lightly

THE NIGHT BEFORE MAKE THE ICE CREAM

1. Preheat the oven to 180°C (gas 4). Place 1½ cups (205 g) hazelnuts (for the ice cream and cookies) on a tray and roast with the skins on for about 10 minutes, until fragrant and the skins loosen, being careful not to let them burn. Remove from the oven and tip into a clean tea towel. Fold over and rub together to remove the skins. Let cool. Set aside ½ cup (70 g) hazelnuts for the cookies tomorrow.

2. Blend the hazelnuts and the rest of the ice cream ingredients until smooth in a food processor. Pour into an airtight container and freeze overnight.

THE NEXT DAY MAKE THE HAZELNUT COOKIES

1. Preheat the oven to 180°C (gas 4). Line a baking tray with baking paper. Place the reserved hazelnuts in a food processor and blitz into a very fine meal. Combine the oil, stevia and vanilla in a large bowl. Add the fresh hazelnut meal, almond meal, salt, half of the whisked egg and mix with a spoon to form dough.

2. Roll out the dough to about 1.5 cm thick. Cut into shapes with a 4–5 cm cookie cutter. Transfer to the prepared tray and brush lightly with the remaining whisked egg to give it a pretty gloss. Bake for 6–8 minutes, until lightly browned around the edges. Cool on the tray.

3. Serve a spoonful of ice cream between two crispy cookies or on top of a couple of raw cookie rounds.

> ### TRICKY TIP
>
> If you'd prefer your dough raw, flatten mixture onto a lined baking tray and store in the fridge for a couple of hours to set. Once set take out and cut with a scone cutter into rounds.

AUSSIE MANGO COCONUT BARS

MAKES 4–6

PREPARATION TIME
5 hours

⅓ cup (35 g) desiccated coconut

1 x 400 ml can coconut cream

1 tablespoon rice malt syrup

1 cup (175 g) diced frozen mango

1. Blend the desiccated coconut, coconut cream and rice malt syrup in a blender or using a hand-held blender until well combined and pour into 4–6 ice lolly moulds until one-third full. You will have coconut mixture remaining for the next step.

2. Freeze for one hour until just set. Add the mango to the remaining coconut mixture and blend until smooth.

3. Top up the moulds with the mango mixture, insert the sticks and freeze for at least 4 hours.

> **TRICKY TIP**
>
> For some extra crunch add a sprinkle of chopped macadamia nuts after pouring in the mango mixture.

COCONUT ICE

MAKES 16

PREPARATION TIME
10 minutes
(+ 2 hours
chilling)

COOKING TIME
5 minutes

⅔ cup (150 ml) coconut oil

1 x 400 ml can coconut milk

½ cup (125 ml) rice malt syrup

4 cups (400 g) desiccated coconut

pinch of beetroot powder (or natural red food colouring of your choice, see page 133)

1. Grease a 20 cm square cake tin. Line base and sides with baking paper extending 2 cm over the edge of the tin.

2. Place the coconut oil, coconut milk and rice malt syrup in a small saucepan over low heat. Stir until melted and combined well. Remove from the heat and stir in the desiccated coconut. Press half the mixture into the base of the prepared tin. Place in the freezer to help base firm a little.

3. Meanwhile add the beetroot powder to the remaining mixture and combine well until the colour is evenly distributed. Press into the tin on top of the white coconut mixture and place in the fridge for at least 2 hours, or until firm.

4. Remove from tin and trim edges. Cut into 16 large squares or 64 smaller squares.

AUSSIE MANGO COCONUT BARS

AUSSIE LOLLIES

MAKES 8–12

PREPARATION TIME
4 hours

GREEN LAYER

½ avocado

1 cup (50 g) spinach

1 banana

1 cup (250 ml) coconut water

GOLD LAYER

1 cup (175 g) diced frozen mango

1 tablespoon rice malt syrup

1 x 400 ml can coconut cream

1. Blend all the ingredients for the green layer in a blender until smooth.
    Pour the mixture into 8–12 ice lolly moulds and fill halfway. Freeze for
    1–2 hours until firm.

2. Blend all the ingredients for the gold layer in a blender until smooth.
    Pour the mixture into moulds on top of the green layer and freeze for
    a further 1–2 hours until the lollies are frozen.

BIRTHDAY SPACE CAKE

This cake can have up to four layers and requires a total of eight eggs. It may seem a lot but it serves 14. That equates to just over half an egg per serve. Allow the kids to enjoy a colourful slice as a special treat.

SERVES 14

PREPARATION TIME
30 minutes

COOKING TIME
65 minutes

BASIC SPONGE (this amount will be sufficient for 3 layers)

400g butter, plus extra for greasing

½ cup (125 ml) rice malt syrup

1 tablespoon granulated stevia

8 eggs

400 g self-raising flour

3 x A Dash of Colour (see page 133)

CREAM CHEESE FROSTING

500 g cream cheese, softened

125 g butter, softened

4 tablespoons rice malt syrup

grated zest and juice of 1 lemon

raw cacao powder or chia seeds, to serve

TO MAKE THE SPONGE

1. Preheat the oven to 170°C. Grease the sides of three 20 cm springform tins and line the bases with baking paper. You can bake the cakes in batches if you only have one or two tins.

2. Melt the butter, syrup and stevia in a small saucepan over low heat – do not boil – then transfer to a measuring jug and set aside to cool slightly. You should have 600 ml of liquid.

3. Beat the eggs until light and fluffy, and doubled in size, using an electric mixer. Set aside.

4. Sift the flour into a large bowl. Transfer one-third of the flour (around 130 g) to a large bowl. Add 200 ml of the butter and syrup mixture (if using berries for colouring, blend them into the liquid before pouring), mix well.

5. Add one-third of the beaten eggs and A Dash of Colour. Whisk well until combined. Pour the batter into the prepared tin. Bake for 20 minutes or until a skewer inserted into the middle of the cake comes out clean. Repeat with the remaining layers and colours. If you can bake all three layers at the same time, you can mix all three batches at once.

6. Remove the cakes from the oven and cool in the tins for 5 minutes before transferring to a wire rack to cool completely.

TO MAKE THE FROSTING

1. Cream all the ingredients using an electric mixer until light and fluffy.

TO ASSEMBLE THE CAKE

1. Place the first layer on a serving plate. Using a spatula spread the frosting around the edges and a thin layer on top. Repeat the process with all three layers.

2. Ice the top of the cake, in a swirling motion to form craters. Sprinkle around the craters with cacao powder or chia seeds. Mount fun figurines on top or around the cake.

RASPBERRY SPIDERS

SERVES 4

PREPARATION TIME
15 minutes
(+ 5 hours
freezing)

3 cups (750 ml) soda water or natural mineral water

shaved coconut (optional), to serve

RASPBERRY DRINK

4 cups (500 ml) raspberries, fresh or frozen

flesh of 1 coconut, blitzed in a food processor (optional)

1 cup (250 ml) water or coconut water from the coconut, if using

SIMPLE COCONUT ICE CREAM

1 x 400 ml can coconut cream

1 tablespoon rice malt syrup

½ teaspoon vanilla powder

TO MAKE THE ICE CREAM

1. Mix all of the ingredients in a blender, or using a hand-held blender, until smooth and creamy. Pour into a freezer-safe container (a lunch box will do) and leave in the freezer for 5 hours, stirring every hour to ensure the mixture remains creamy. Alternatively use an ice cream maker, if you have one.

TO MAKE THE RASPBERRY DRINK

1. Place the raspberries, coconut flesh, if using, and water in a blender or food processor. Blend on high until smooth to make a puree.

TO ASSEMBLE

1. Place 4 tablespoons of the raspberry puree in each of four glasses and slowly add the soda or mineral water and stir until combined.

2. Top with a scoop or two of the Simple Coconut Ice Cream. Sprinkle with shaved coconut if you like.

> ### TRICKY TIP
>
> Store the remaining puree in an airtight container in the fridge and the leftover ice cream in the freezer.

EGGSHELL BROWNIES

This recipe is a great showstopper! The novelty of peeling back the eggshells to reveal a chocolate brownie will have the kids bursting with excitement. Make this dish at Easter rather than loading the kids up with cheap and nasty store-bought guff.

MAKES 12

PREPARATION TIME
15 minutes

COOKING TIME
25 minutes

12 eggs

1 cup (250 ml) Pumpkin Puree (see page 23)

⅓ cup (75 ml) milk or coconut milk

4 tablespoons rice malt syrup

4 tablespoons coconut oil, melted

2 teaspoons vanilla powder

⅓ cup (40 g) coconut flour

4 tablespoons raw cacao powder

2 teaspoons baking powder

1 teaspoon bicarbonate of soda

4 tablespoons macadamia nuts, roughly chopped

1. Preheat the oven to 170°C (gas 3).

2. Using the pointy end of a sharp knife, pierce the top of 12 eggshells and peel back enough shell so that the opening is big enough to pipe brownie batter into. Shake contents of 10 of the eggs into a bowl to refrigerate for later, and two into a smaller bowl for use now.

3. Lay crumpled aluminium foil in a cupcake tin, forming a base to stand the eggs. Wash shells thoroughly under cold running water. Place the prepared eggshells in the cupcake tin.

4. Place the Pumpkin Puree, milk, syrup and coconut oil in a small saucepan over low heat. Cook, stirring until the mixture is melted and combined. Remove from the heat and set aside to cool slightly. Add the vanilla powder to the reserved eggs and beat using an electric beater until light and fluffy.

5. Mix the flour, cacao, baking powder, bicarbonate of soda and macadamias in a large bowl. Add the pumpkin mixture and beaten eggs then stir to combine. Transfer the mixture to a piping bag fitted with a 1 cm round nozzle. Pipe the batter into the prepared eggshells to about three-quarters full. Bake for 15–20 minutes or until a skewer inserted through the hole comes out clean.

No wastage here!
If you're concerned with the waste of eggs don't be. Two of these eggs will go into the batter and the rest can be used in quiche, omelettes, and other breakfasts. Alternatively freeze eggs in portions and simply thaw when you need them for a recipe.

A DASH OF COLOUR

Kids love colours! Yes! But rather than sending them super-charged crazy on artificial colours, there are some great natural alternatives to colour your cakes and frostings.

COLOUR	INGREDIENT & METHOD
Blue	Juiced or blended and strained frozen blueberries
Green	Juiced spinach leaves or a dash of chlorophyll
Red	Juiced or blended and strained frozen raspberries
Pink	Juiced beetroots
Yellow	Pinch of saffron or turmeric mixed into a dash of boiling water
Orange	Juiced carrots
Purple	The juice from a cut and boiled red cabbage

TRICKY TIP

Dye desiccated coconut an assortment of colours by popping it in a ziplock bag with natural colourings you've already made, and use the freshly coloured coconut as 'sprinkles'!

A LIST OF STUDIES AND SOURCES

Pages vi–7

Sugar consumption in children.
www.life.familyeducation.com/nutritional-information/obesity/64270.html

Sugar alters the palate.
http://www.ncbi.nlm.nih.gov/pmc/articles/PMC4500487/

Sugar is linked to childhood obesity.
https://www.sciencedaily.com/releases/2013/08/130805112854.htm

Sugar is linked to childhood aggression.
www.healthland.time.com/2013/08/16/soda-contributes-to-behavior-problems-among-young-children/

Sugary drinks may damage children's memory.
http://www.medicaldaily.com/sugary-drinks-may-damage-childrens-brains-so-badly-it-affects-their-memory-295558

Soft Drinks Consumption is Associated with Behavior Problems in Five-Year Olds.
www.crcw.princeton.edu/workingpapers/WP13–10–FF.pdf

Australian dietary guidelines.
http://www.nhmrc.gov.au/_files_nhmrc/publications/attachments/n55f_children_brochure.pdf

USA dietary guidelines.
http://health.gov/dietaryguidelines/

UK dietary guidelines.
https://www.gov.uk/government/publications/the-eatwell-guide

Study on cooking initiative in Liverpool.
http://www.cancook.co.uk/wp-content/uploads/2012/01/Report-on-a-Cooking-Initiative-in-Liverpool-a-study-of-the-activities-of-Can-Cook.pdf

Study by the School Food Trust.
www.childrensfoodtrust.org.uk/assets/research-reports/LGC_Big_Lottery_Evaluation_Summary_Report_A4_24pp_WEB.pdf

INDEX

THANK YOU

The I Quit Sugar Kids' Cookbook was put together by the I Quit Sugar team. Thanks to the Pan Macmillan team and the fantastic food photography and styling that was carried out by Rob Palmer and Bernie Smithies.

Special mention goes out to our contributors and readers who kindly shared their favourite recipes. We hope this kids' book inspires you to get your kids into the kitchen and cooking away by your side.

First published 2016 by Pan Macmillan Australia Pty Ltd

First published in the UK 2017 by Bluebird
an imprint of Pan Macmillan
20 New Wharf Road, London N1 9RR
Associated companies throughout the world
www.panmacmillan.com

ISBN 978-1-5098-4369-5

A CIP catalogue record for this book is available from the British Library.

Design by Elissa Webb, adapted from design by Lisa Valuyskaya
Printed in China

Food styling and props by Bernadette Smithies
Food preparation by Sarah Mayoh

Visit **www.panmacmillan.com** to read more about all our books and to buy them. You will also find features, author interviews and news of any author events, and you can sign up for e-newsletters so that you're always first to hear about our new releases.